Universal Humanitarian Wisdom

A DIALOGUE BETWEEN THE GOD AND DEVOTEE

Dr. O P Adarsh

The voice of the soul is the voice of God. Recognizing and following the instructions of the divine while riding the chariot of the body is the essence of human spirituality.

-Om Shri

ISBN
Paperback 979-8-89498-377-6
Hardcase 979-8-89498-889-4

About the Author

Born on 3rd March 1971, Dr. Om Prakash 'Adarsh' completed his schooling in his birth place Barauli, Gopalganj (Bihar). He comes from a middle-class, highly religious, and vegetarian family.

Having pledged to donate his whole body and the same of his family's, he is a doctor who completed his MBBS from Darbhanga Medical college and has an MBA in Hospital Administration.

He has worked in AIIMS, Safdarjung Hospital, Max Hospital, Delhi Govt. Hospital and received a Certificate of Appreciation from Central Govt. Health Ministry.

Another spiritual book by the author: *Vishwa Sanatan Manav Dharm* (in Hindi)

Contact: dropg73@gmail.com

Oh Mother Saraswati

____

Universal Humanitarian Wisdom

(A Dialogue between The God and Devotee)

Knowledge of Realization

By

Dr. Om Prakash 'Adarsh'

(Om Shri)

Published with the requisite support of my wife
Shephali Prakash.

Dedicated to Society – The Global Village

It is a good thing to love your country; but it is a
greater thing to love all of humanity.

To abandon one's duty is ignorance.

Renunciation is the giving up of attachment to the fruits of action. It is religion (righteousness) to perform one's duties while living in one's own society.

My Thoughts

In some of the available translated texts of Shrimad Bhagavad Gita, there is less devotion and more knowledge and one gets tired while reading them and is unable to understand the basic point completely. On the other hand, in some texts, the feeling of devotion is so much that one is unable to reach the end after reading it completely, due to which the understanding of knowledge remains less.

By the grace of God, due to all those reasons, initially for my own help, I wrote the understanding of Shrimad Bhagavad Gita in the simplest colloquial language and in easy words of current times with necessary explanation, in which I tried to properly coordinate knowledge, devotion and action. But now, by God's grace, I thought why not give this to other needy people in the society so that they can also benefit from it and get the strength and understanding to live. With this auspicious purpose in mind this book is being published. This book has taken the kind cooperation of Gita Mata written by Mahatma Gandhi, Dr. Sarvepalli Radhakrishnan's translation on Bhagavad Gita, Sri Bhaktivedanta Swami Prabhupada's translation of Srimad Bhagavad Gita as it is and Srimad Bhagavad Gita of Gita Press and does not neglect any translated text. May the help of Maa Saraswati and the blessings of Lord Shri Bhagwan remain on everyone.

Dr. O. P. Adarsh

New Delhi

Knowledge and Understanding of the Eternal Human Religion (Righteousness)

Preface

Srimad Bhagavad Gita is the essence of all the greatest spiritual texts which have been passed down from ancient times for the welfare of all mankind.

Not only does it contain the ways of life written in all the religious scriptures of the world, it also contains things other than that and all of them have been proved in every way. For the person who takes help of this book, there is no room for despair and he always remains blissful.

By understanding the thing which we want to use all the time and with the help of which we try to solve all our internal problems, in as many ways and in whatever way it can be understood, and by meditating on it again and again, we ultimately become absorbed to do our duty.

There is no such problem in life for which Geeta cannot help in its solution. There is a wonderful co-ordination of knowledge, devotion and action in it and human life is based on these three foundations.

The Gita is a small but main section of the enormous Mahabharata. Mahabharata and Ramayana are based on historical events which have been transformed into spiritual texts that are the realization of our own soul's battle for the victory of good over evil that is constantly going on in every human body.

Geeta, written in Sanskrit, is a great religious poem, which is the enlightenment given by Shri Krishna to Arjun, which has been sung since ancient times and is passed on.

We know the voice of our conscience. The voice of conscience is the voice of God. We should read the Gita with the understanding that the omniscient Lord Shri Krishna is present in our body as a charioteer and when we become inquisitive Arjun and ask the omniscient Lord in a religious crisis and seek His refuge, then we will find Him ready to give us refuge.

Mahatma Gandhi writes that it is we who are asleep, but the inner self is always awake. They always wait for the time when curiosity arises in us, but we do not know how to ask a question, the thought of asking a question does not even come to mind. For this reason, we daily meditate on the great scripture of human religion in the form of the Gita. While singing its praises, we desire to generate religious curiosity in our minds. We want to learn to ask questions. Whenever we are in trouble, we take refuge in the Gita and get assurance from it. We have to read this scripture with this view in mind. This is the form of our spiritual guru, and we must believe that by seeking refuge in this form, we will navigate through life safely and find solutions to all our religious dilemmas through this scripture. There is not a single religious problem which this book cannot solve. If our lack of faith causes us to lose interest in reading and understanding, that's one thing. However, we should read and reflect on this scripture regularly to strengthen our faith and stay vigilant.

Failure in behavior happens on a daily basis, but it is part of our ongoing efforts. In this failure, a glimpse of the emerging rays of success is visible.

May everyone's life be successful through knowledge, good deeds and devotion to God.

In the name of God.

Dr. O. P. Adarsh

New Delhi

The Teachings of the Bhagavad Gita as Interpreted by Mahatma Gandhi

The Shrimadbhagavad Gita describes the ongoing battle within the hearts of all individuals, using physical war as a metaphor. The creation of human warriors in the mythological tale was created to make the war of hearts interesting. This initial inspiration solidified after carefully considering religion and the teachings of the Gita. After reading Mahabharata this thought became even stronger. I do not consider the Mahabharata text to be history in the modern sense. Strong evidence of this is found in the Adi Parva itself. By describing the inhuman and superhuman origin of the characters, Lord Vyas has erased the history of the king and his subjects. The characters described in it may be historical in origin, but in the Mahabharata, Lord Vyas has used them only to give the philosophy of religion.

The author of Mahabharata has proved not the need for physical war but its futility. The victor has been made to cry, repent and be left with nothing but sorrow.

Geeta resides in the pre-eminent form in this great book. Its second chapter, instead of teaching physical warfare practices, teaches the characteristics of a person possessing steady wisdom. It is clear to me from his traits that a person who possesses steady wisdom is not involved in worldly conflicts. It is not possible to write a book like the Gita to judge the appropriateness or inappropriateness of ordinary family disputes.

Krishna of Gita is pure complete knowledge personified. But they are imaginary. There is no denying the existence of the incarnate person named Krishna. Only the complete Krishna is imaginary, the imposition of the complete incarnation was done later.

Incarnation refers to the tangible appearance of a distinct individual. All living beings are incarnations of God, but in worldly language, we do not call everyone an incarnation. The man who is the most religious man of his age is worshiped by the future generations as an incarnation. I don't see any fault in this. In this neither the greatness of God is diminished nor the truth is harmed. "A person is not God; but a person is not separate from the light of God." The one in whom religious awakening is the highest in his era is a special incarnation. According to this belief, the full embodiment of Krishna is currently enjoying his reign in Hinduism today.

This scene is indicative of man's last good wish. Man cannot find comfort or peace without becoming God-like. Becoming God-like is the only real effort, which leads to self-realization. All religious texts focus on the concept of self-awareness, and the same is true for the teachings of the Gita. But the author of the Gita did not write it to explain this topic; rather, the intention of the Gita is to provide the self-seeker with a unique way of self-realization. Whatever is seen scattered in the scriptures of Sanatan Dharma, has been well established by the Gita in many forms and in many words, even while admitting the fault of repetition.

That unique solution is 'renunciation of the fruits of action.'

The entire focus of the Gita's decoration revolves around this central point. Devotion, knowledge etc. are decorated around it in the form of a constellation. Wherever there is body, there is action. Every person is subject to it, but all religions teach that by treating the body as a sacred place, one can achieve salvation. However, there is always some imperfection in every action; true salvation is only achieved by the innocent. Then how can one be freed from the bondage of karma, that is, from the touch of faults? Geeta answers this in definite words - "By doing selfless work, by doing work for the sake of sacrifice, by renouncing the fruits of action, by dedicating all actions to Krishna, that is, by sacrificing the mind, speech and body to God."

But desirelessness and renunciation of the fruits of action cannot be achieved merely by saying it. This is not just the use of intellect. This arises only from churning of the heart. To develop this power of sacrifice, knowledge is required. Many scholars attain one type of knowledge. They know the Vedas by heart, but most of them remain engrossed in worldly pleasures. The author of the Gita prioritized a combination of devotion and knowledge to prevent excessive knowledge from becoming mere academic learning. Knowledge without devotion is harmful. This is the reason behind the saying, "Engage in devotion and you will undoubtedly attain wisdom." However, devotion requires intellectual understanding, which is why the author of the Geeta has portrayed devotion as having the qualities of a person with stable wisdom.

Meaning, the devotion of Gita is not externalism, it is not blind faith. The remedies mentioned in the Gita have minimal connection with any external gesture or action. Though devotees may use means like garland, Tilak etc., they are not the signs of devotion. One who does not hate anyone, who is a treasury of compassion and is devoid of attachment, who is selfless, to whom happiness and sorrow, cold and heat are the same, who is forgiving, who is always satisfied, whose decisions never change, who has dedicated his mind and intellect to God, who does not agitate people, who does not fear people, who is free from joy, sorrow and fear, who is pure, who is neutral despite being efficient, who renounces good and bad, who has equal respect for friends and enemies, who is equal to respect and insult, who does not feel happy with praise and does not feel ashamed with criticism, who is silent, who loves solitude, who has a steady mind, is a devotee. This devotion is not possible among attached men and women.

From this, we see that attaining knowledge and becoming a devotee is self-realization. Self-realization is not different from this. Unlike how poison and nectar can be obtained with money, it is not possible to attain bondage and liberation through knowledge or devotion. Here, the means and the end are, if not exactly the same, then almost the same thing; the culmination of the means is Moksha (salvation), and the meaning of Moksha in the Gita is ultimate peace.

But such knowledge and devotion has to stand the test of renunciation of the fruits of action. In worldly imagination, even a dry scholar is considered to be knowledgeable. He has no work to do. Even lifting the pot with his hands is a bondage of karma for him. Where a person is considered wise without any sacrifice, how can a trivial worldly act like picking up a small pot find a place there?

In worldly imagination, devotee means an external follower, one who chants with a rosary. Even while performing service, there is distraction in his rosary. Therefore, he keeps the rosary away from his hand only when he eats or drinks and never when he works at the grinder or tends to sick person.

To both these groups, the Gita clearly said, "Without action, no one has achieved success. Janaka and others also became knowledgeable through their actions. If I too do not keep performing my duties without laziness, then these worlds will be destroyed." Then what is left for people to ask?

But on one hand, it is indisputable that all karmas are a form of bondage. On the other hand, the soul continues to perform actions willingly or unwillingly. All efforts, physical or mental, are karma. Then how can a man remain free from bondage even while performing his duties? As far as I know, no other religious text has solved this problem the way the Gita has. The Gita says, "Give up attachment to results and do your work", "Do your work without any expectation", "Do your work without any desire." This is the message of the Gita which cannot be forgotten. He who abandons action, falls. He who abandons the fruits of his actions while performing them, ascends. Renunciation of the fruit does not mean being careless about the outcome. The consideration and knowledge of the result and the means is essential. After all this, the person who remains engrossed in the means without desiring the result is a renunciator of the result.

But here, no one should interpret renunciation of the fruit to mean that the one who renounces does not get the fruit at all. There is no place for such a meaning in the Gita. By renunciation of fruit means the absence of attachment to the fruit. In reality, the one who renounces fruit gets a thousand times the benefits. There is a test of infinite faith in the renunciation of the fruit of the Gita. A person who keeps thinking about the outcome often corrupts his duties. He is frustrated and impatient, which leads to anger, causing him to engage in inappropriate behavior as he moves from one action to another, and then to a third. The person who worries about the result becomes like a person blind to the subject. In the end, like a sensualist, he gives up the discrimination of right and wrong, and uses any means to obtain the result and considers it as Dharma.

From such bitter consequences of attachment to results, the author of Geeta derived the principle of non-attachment I.e. renunciation of the results of actions and presented it to the world in a very attractive language. Generally, it is believed that Dharma and Artha (righteousness and business) are opposite things, "Dharma cannot be saved in worldly dealings like business etc., Dharma cannot have a place, Dharma can be used only for Moksha (salvation). Dharma looks good in place of Dharma and Artha looks good in place of Artha." We hear many people saying this. The author of Geeta has removed this misconception. He has not made any distinction between salvation and conduct, but has brought religion into conduct. The religion which cannot be put into practice is not a religion, in my understanding, this is what the Gita states. Meaning, according to the Gita, all those actions which cannot be performed without attachment are to be avoided. Such a golden rule saves a person from many religious dilemmas. According to this belief, acts like murder, lying, adultery etc. automatically become condemnable. Human life becomes simple and simplicity gives rise to peace.

According to this line of thought, it seems to me that the one who puts the teachings of the Gita into practice automatically has to follow truth and non-violence. Without attachment to results, a man is neither tempted to tell a lie nor to commit violence. Whatever act of violence or untruth we take, it will be known that behind it there is a desire for consequences. Even before the Gita era, non-violence was considered the ultimate form of religion, but the Gita had to propound the principle of detachment. This becomes clear in the second chapter itself.

But if the Gita accepted nonviolence, or if nonviolence comes automatically in detachment, then why did the author of the Gita take physical war as an example? In the era of Gita, even though non-violence was considered a religion, physical war being a universally accepted thing, the author of Gita did not hesitate to take the example of such a war and he shouldn't have.

But, understanding the importance of renunciation of the fruits of action, we do not need to think about what the author of the Gita had in mind and where he had set the limits of non-violence. The poet presents important principles to the world, but this does not mean that he always recognizes the principles he presents as important or that after recognizing them he is able to put them all into language. There is glory of poetry and poet in this. There is no end to the poet's meaning. Just like a human being, the meaning of the great sentences keeps on evolving. From the history of languages, we learn that the meanings of many great words have been constantly changing. The same thing is true regarding the meaning of Gita. The author of Geeta himself has expanded the meaning of great conventional words. This fact becomes evident even by looking at the Gita superficially. Before the Gita era, animal slaughter may have been acceptable in yagya. But there is not even a trace of it in the yagya of Geeta. In the text, Japayajna is the king of all yajnas. The third chapter explains that yajna primarily means the use of the body for charity. By combining the third and fourth chapters, other interpretations can be derived, but animal cruelty cannot be derived. The same thing is true regarding the meaning of renunciation in the Gita. Renunciation of mere action does not appeal to the renunciation mentioned in the Gita. The Sannyasi of the Gita is over-active, yet over-inactive. In this way, by giving a broader meaning to the great words, the writer of Geeta has taught us to give a broader meaning to our language as well.

O Lord Rama…

Contents

Words of wisdom to help in the internal battle
by using the external battle as an illustration.

A Dialogue Between the God and Devotee

1. Arjuna Visada Yoga (Good Person in Suffering)

1. Dhritarashtra said -

   Hey Sanjay! Tell me, what did my and Pandu's sons, assembled in the battlefield of Kurukshetra, which was like the battlefield of Dharma, with the desire to fight, do?

   Kauravas mean bad tendencies, Pandavas mean good tendencies. This body-like area is the area of Dharma. What is good and what is bad - curious people keep churning their hearts about this.

2. Sanjay said -

   At that time, seeing the Pandava army ready, King Duryodhan went to Acharya Drona and said-

3. O Acharya, look at this large army of the Pandavas prepared by your intelligent disciple, Dhristadyumna, son of Drupada.

4. Standing here are skilled warriors like Bhima, Arjuna, archer Yuyudhana (Satyaki), Virata and the great charioteer Drupadaraja,

5. Dhrishtaketu, Chekitana, great warrior Kasiraja, Purujit, Kutimbhoja and Shaibya, the best of men,

6. Similarly, the mighty Yudhamanyu the gallant Uttammauja, the son of Subhadra (Abhimanyu) and the son of Draupadi, all of them are great warriors.

7. O best of the Brāhmaṇas! Now you should know the main warriors on our side. I ask you to bring to your attention the names of the heroes of our army.

8. One is you, Bhishma, Karna, Kripacharya, the victorious in battle, Ashvatthama, Vikarna and Somadatta's son Bhurisrava,

9. There are many others too who are brave warriors fighting with various kinds of weapons and are ready to sacrifice their lives for me. They are all skilled in war.

10. The strength of our army protected by Bhishma is incomplete, but his army protected by Bhima is complete.

11. Therefore, all of you should protect Bhishma Pitamah well from your respective places and from all routes. (Thus said Duryodhana)

12. Then, to cheer him up, the old and glorious grandfather of Kuru roared loudly and blew his conch.

13. Then the conches, kettledrums, drums, mridangas and war horns started playing simultaneously. This sound was terrible.

14. Meanwhile, Sri Krishna and Arjuna, seated on a huge chariot drawn by white horses, blew their divine conches.

15. Shri Krishna blew the Panchjanya conch. Dhananjaya Arjuna blew the Devadatta conch. Bhima, who performed terrible deeds, blew the great conch called Paundra.

16. King Yudhisthira, son of Kunti, blew the conch named Anantavijaya, Nakula blew the conch named Sughosha and Sahadeva blew the conch named Manipushpaka.

17. King of Kashi with a big bow, great warrior Shikhandi, Ghristhadyumna, King of Virata, invincible Satyaki,

18. King of Drupada, the son of Draupadi, the mighty-armed Abhimanyu, the son of Subhadra, all of them, O King! Everyone blew their conches.

19. That terrible sound, which reverberated through the earth and the sky, impaled the hearts of the Kauravas.

20. O King! Arjuna, bearing the flag bearing the symbol of Hanuman, seeing the Kauravas arrayed himself, drew his bow and while preparing to shoot, spoke these words to Hrishikesha:

21. "O Achyuta Krishna! Place my chariot between the two armies.

22. So that I can see the people standing with the desire for war and know with whom I have to fight in this battle.

23. Let me see the warriors who wish to see the evil-minded Duryodhana win the war."

24-25. Sanjay said -

O King! When Arjuna said this to Shri Krishna, he stationed a great chariot in the middle of both the armies in front of all the kings and Bhishma-Drona and said - "O Partha! Look at these assembled Kauravas."

26-27. Arjuna saw the elders, grandfathers, teachers, maternal uncles, brothers, sons, grandsons, friends, fathers-in-law and loved ones present in both armies. Seeing all his relatives standing like this, feeling sad due to regret, the son of Kunti spoke thus-

28-29. O Krishna! Looking at these relatives and friends gathered eagerly for the war, my body is getting weak, my mouth is getting dry, my body is trembling and has goosebumps.

30. Gandiva is slipping from the hand, the skin is burning. I cannot stand anymore, as my mind is getting confused.

31. Apart from this, O Keshav! I am seeing opposite symptoms. I see no benefit in killing one's own relatives in war.

32. O Krishna! By killing them I neither want victory nor kingdom and happiness; O Govinda! What do I need the kingdom, the pleasures of life, or the world for that matter?

33-34. Those for whom we have desired kingdom, enjoyment and happiness, those very teachers, uncles, sons, grandfathers, maternal uncles, fathers-in-law, grandsons, brothers-in-law and other relatives have given up hope of life and wealth and are standing for the war.

35. Therefore, O Madhusudana! Even if they kill me or I get the kingdom of the three worlds, I do not want to kill them. Then how do I kill for a piece of land?

36. O Janardana! What pleasure will I get by killing the sons of Dhritarashtra? We would be committing a sin by killing these tyrants.

37. Therefore, O Madhava! It is not right that we kill the sons of our own uncle Dhritarashtra. Because how can we be happy by killing our own people (relatives)?

38-39. Those whose minds have become impure due to greed may not be able to see the fault that results from the destruction of the family and the sin of betraying a friend, but O Janardana! why shouldn't we, who understand the evil that results from the destruction of a clan, avoid this sin?

40. With the destruction of a clan, the eternal clan principles are destroyed, and with the destruction of Dharma, unrighteousness drowns the entire clan.

    Sanatan = always lasting, that is, which has no beginning and no end.

    Dharma = duty with good sense

    Kul = entire extended family

41. O Krishna! With the increase of sin, the women of the family become corrupted and due to their corruption, a hybrid caste is born.

    hybrid = mixed

42. Due to a hybrid caste, the destroyer of the clan and, through him, the clan goes to hell, and

being deprived of the ritual of Pindodaka, his forefathers suffer degradation.

Hell for the family = loss of respect for the family

Pindodaka ritual = A ritual performed for the dead ancestors which has the effect of bringing peace to the mind.

43. The defects which cause this hybridisation of the clan-destroyer people, lead to the destruction of their Sanatana Dharma and the clan-religions.

44. O Janardana! We have heard that a person whose family religion is destroyed definitely goes to hell.

    Naraka = to be lower than the eyes = to lose respect

    Heaven = being above the eyelids = increase in respect

45. Oh! How sad it is that we have become inclined to commit great sins, that is, for the greed of the pleasures of rule, we have become ready to kill our own relatives.

46. If the armed sons of Dhritarashtra kill me, who is unarmed and unable to face them, in a battle, that will be very beneficial for me.

47. Sanjay said -

Saying this, Arjuna, distraught with grief in the battle, put down his bow and arrows and sat in the rear part of the chariot.

2. Sankhya Yoga

1. Sanjay said -

    Thus, Madhusudan Krishna said these words to Arjun who was sad and had tearful eyes and was depressed with compassion -

2. The Lord said -

    O Arjun! How did you come to develop this unworthy attachment, that detracts from your greatness, leads you away from heaven, and brings shame during a challenging period?

3. O Partha! Don't become impotent. This does not suit you. Abandoning all petty weakness of the heart, O Arjuna! get up.

4. Arjun said -

    O Madhusudan! How can I kill Bhishma and Drona with arrows on the battlefield? O

Destroyer of demons, Krishna! They are worthy of worship.

5. It is better to eat alms in this world than to kill the teachers because after killing the teachers I will have to enjoy wealth and pleasures in the form of lust soaked in blood.

6. And we do not even know what is best for us to do, or whether we will win or they will win over us, and those very sons of Dhritarashtra, whom we do not want to kill and even live, are standing before us.

7. Due to cowardice I am not able to perform my natural duties. I have become confused about my duties. Therefore, I request you to tell me with certainty whatever is in my interest. I am your disciple. I have come to your shelter. Please show me the way.

8. Even if I get a trouble-free kingdom full of wealth and prosperity on this earth and the throne of Lord Indra, I do not see how my sorrow, which is drying up the senses, would go away.

9. Sanjay said -

O King! Gudakesh Arjun became silent after saying this to Rishikesh Govind, 'I will not fight.'

10. After this, O Bharata! In the midst of the two armies, the all-knowing Sri Krishna Maharaj gently spoke these words to the sorrowful Arjun with a smile on his face.

11. Shri Bhagwan said -

    You mourn for what is not worth mourning for and speak words of wisdom; but scholars do not mourn for the dead or the living.

    pandit = scholar

12. Because, looking at the reality, neither I, nor you, nor these kings existed at some time, nor will exist in the future, there is no such thing because the Soul is eternal.

13. Just as a being gets bodies of youth, young age and old age in this body, similarly he gets other bodies as well. A patient man is not attracted by this.

14. O son of Kunti! The touch of the senses that give us cold and heat and happiness and sorrow are temporary, therefore, O Arjuna, descendant of Bharata! You tolerate them.

15. O best of men! The patient man who remains the same in pleasure and pain and is not troubled by the objects of the senses becomes eligible for salvation.

16. Falsehood does not exist and truth does not perish. The decision regarding both of these is known to wise men.

17. That by which this entire universe is pervaded, know it to be indestructible. Because no one is capable of destroying this indestructible one.

18. These bodies of the eternally existing, infinite and indestructible soul are said to be destructible; therefore, O Arjuna, descendant of Bharata! You fight the war.

19. He who thinks that this soul can be killed and he who believes that it is dead, neither know because this soul neither dies nor is killed.

20. It is never born, it never dies. It is not like this was there and will not be in the future. Therefore, it is unborn, eternal, everlasting, and ancient; it does not get destroyed with the destruction of the body.

21. O son of Pritha! The man who believes the soul to be indestructible, eternal, unborn and unbreakable, whom does he get killed and how, or whom does he kill?

22. And if you say that I mourn the separation from the bodies, then this also is wrong; because just as a man discards old clothes and wears new

ones, similarly the soul discards the old body and gets another new body.

23. This soul cannot be pierced by weapons, cannot be burnt by fire, cannot be wet by water and cannot be dried by air.

24. This soul cannot be pierced, burnt, soaked or dried. It is eternal, omnipresent, stable, unshakable and everlasting.

25. This soul cannot be reached by the senses and the mind; therefore, it is said to be without any sin. Knowing it to be so, it is not proper for you to grieve.

26. Or even if you consider him to be continually born and dying, O mighty-armed one! It is not right for you to mourn.

27. Death is inevitable for the born and birth is inevitable for the dead. Therefore, it is not appropriate to grieve over something that is inevitable.

28. O Bharata! All living beings are without body before birth and even after death they are without body; in between they appear to have body, then what is the worry in this matter?

29. Some see this Soul as a wonder and some hear it described as a wonder, but even after hearing about it, no one knows it.

30. O Bharata! This soul is always indestructible in everyone's body; therefore, it is not appropriate for you to mourn for all living beings.

31. Even after understanding your duty, it is not right for you to hesitate; because no other auspicious duty can be more beneficial for a Kshatriya than a righteous war.

    Kshatriya = A person with the nature of fighting against evil and protecting the good.

32. O Partha! A war that was achieved opportunity automatically and as if the doors to heaven had opened up is experienced only by fortunate Kshatriyas.

33. And if you do not fight this righteous war, you will lose your religious duty and fame and will commit sin.

34. And everyone will keep on criticizing you for a long time and for a respected man, disgrace is worse than death.

35. And those great warriors from whom you have received respect will consider you to have fled from the battle out of fear and will consider you to be insignificant.

36. And your enemies will say many unspeakable things, criticizing your power. What could be more painful than this?

37. If you die you will get heaven and if you win you will enjoy the earth. Therefore, O son of Kunti! You stand up, determined to fight.

38. Consider happiness and sorrow, profit and loss, victory and defeat as equal and prepare for the battle. You will not commit any sin by fighting in this manner.

39. I have told you about your duty according to the Sankhya theory. Now listen, I will explain it to you according to Karma yoga. By taking shelter of this you will be able to break the bondage of karma.

40. In this way, while attempting to perform one's duty the beginning is not destroyed nor does it lead to the opposite result. Even a little observance of this righteousness saves one from great fear.

41. O Kurunandana! Those who follow this path of performing their duties have a uniform, determined intellect; but those who do not follow this path, the intellects of such indecisive people, are multi-branched and endless.

42-43. Men of limited knowledge are overly attached to those flowery words of the Vedas which speak of performing actions with a view to obtaining various fruits such as attainment of heaven, good birth, power, etc.

44. The wisdom of those who are addicted to pleasures and luxuries is lost. Their wisdom is neither determined nor does it remain stable in meditation.

    Samadhi = controlled mind

45. O Arjun! You should remain detached from the three qualities which are the subject of the Vedas. Be free from the dualities of happiness and sorrow. Always remain steadfast in the truth. Be free from the hassles of obtaining and handling anything and become self-reliant.

46. Just as all the things that come out of a well, come out of the lake in every way, similarly, whatever is in the Vedas is obtained by the knowledgeable and Brahma-devoted person through self-experience.

47. You have the right only to perform the duty, and not to the many fruits that arise from it. The fruit of action is not your purpose. You should not have the urge to not do any work.

48. O Dhananjaya! Having given up attachment and remaining in yoga, that is, by keeping the same attitude towards success and failure, you should perform your duty. Such equanimity is called yoga.

49. O Dhananjaya! Mere action is very insignificant compared to the wisdom of equanimity. You should take shelter of equanimity of mind. People who use the purpose for the result are worthy of pity.

50. A wise man, i.e. a man of equanimity, is not touched by sin and virtue here; therefore, you should strive for equanimity. Efficiency lies in performing one's duty while keeping the mind balanced.

The ultimate wisdom is not to renounce the action, but to renounce the fruits of the action (dispassion from the fruits). This brings stability in the mind. By maintaining detachment from the fruits of duty, one is not touched by sin or virtue.

51. Because, being equanimous intellect, being detached from the results of duty, is freed from the bondage of birth and attains the immaculate state - salvation.

Those whose intellect does not remain stable in equanimity, they repeatedly get dejected and fall below their high mental level. After some time, when you understand your entire situation, you come back to your full mental state. In this way, suffering occurs due to repeated births.

52. When your intellect crosses the mire of attachment, then you will become indifferent both to what you have heard and to what is yet to be heard.

53. When your intellect, agitated by listening to various kinds of doctrines, becomes stable in meditation, only then will you attain equanimity.

54. Having heard the Lord's words thus, Arjuna asked: O Keshava! What are the characteristics of a Sthitaprajna? How does a Sthitaprajna speak, sit and walk?

55. Shri Bhagwan said- O Partha! When a person abandons all the desires arising in his mind (becomes detached) and remains satisfied with the soul through the soul only, then he is called Sthitaprajna.

56. He who is not saddened by sorrow, does not desire happiness, and is free from attachment, fear, and anger is called a sage of steady intellect (a good-minded person).

57. The man who is free from attachment everywhere and neither rejoices nor laments on receiving good or bad, his mind is stable.

58. Just as a tortoise withdraws its limbs from all sides, similarly when a person withdraws his

senses from their objects (withdraws his mind), then his intellect is said to be stable.

59. When a mortal remains without food, his sense-objects become less desirable, but his interest does not go away. That joy ends only when one has a realization of God.

    The only way to ensure that the senses do not stray towards their objects is to have a realization of God. Fasting etc. are measures to slow down these sense-objects.

60. O son of Kunti! The senses are so strong and rapid that they forcibly overpower the mind of even a prudent man who tries to control them.

61. Keeping all these senses under control, the yogi should remain absorbed in Me, because the one who has his senses under control, his intellect is stable.

62. A man who contemplates on worldly objects develops an attachment to them, from attachment arises desire, and from desire arises anger.

    Desire is never satisfied, that is why the person having desire always gets angry.

63. Anger gives rise to indiscretion, and indiscretion confuses the memory, and when the memory

is confused, knowledge is destroyed, and one whose knowledge has been destroyed is like a dead person.

64. But a man whose mind is under his control and whose senses are under his control without any likes or dislikes, attains inner happiness even while enjoying the objects through the senses.

65. The offering of devotion to God results in joy for the soul, which in turn eliminates all sorrows and brings stability to the intellect of the individual who experiences this happiness.

66. One who does not have good intellect does not have good intentions (devotion to God) and one who does not have devotion does not have peace. And where there is no peace, how can there be happiness?

67. Just as the wind pulls a boat in water, similarly, the mind pulls the intellect of a person whose mind runs after the senses wandering in worldly pleasures, wherever it wants.

68. Therefore, O mighty-armed! The person whose senses come under his control after getting free from all the objects, his intellect becomes stable.

69. What is night for all beings is the time of awakening for the self-controlled person, and

what is the time of awakening for all beings is night for the introspective sage.

Just as a person remains unaware of the outside world while sleeping at night, similarly a self-controlled person stays away from worldly affairs and realizes God.

70. The man who is not disturbed by the unceasing flow of desires, like rivers constantly flowing into the ocean, and who remains always calm, is the one who attains peace, not the other who tries to satisfy such desires.

71. A person who renounces all desires for sense gratification and walks without desire, affection and egoism attains peace.

72. O Partha! A person who understands God is no longer under the influence of attachment and if this state remains till the end, then he attains the form of God.

3. Karma Yoga

1. Arjun said- O Janardan! If you consider equanimity of mind to be better than action (sakaam karma), then O Keshav! Why do you force me into doing hard work?

2. Your multiple meaning statements have confused my intellect. Therefore, please tell me definitely one thing which will be of greatest benefit to me.

3. Shri Bhagwan said -

   O sinless one! In this world I have already mentioned two types of devotion - one is that of the Sankhyas through the Yoga of Knowledge, and the other is that of the Yogis through the Yoga of Action.

4. Neither can a man experience inaction by not performing actions nor can he achieve success by abandoning actions.

5. Nor can anyone remain without doing any work even for a moment. Everyone is compelled to act as per the qualities generated by nature.

6. He who restrains the senses from performing actions but continues to think about the objects of those senses in his mind is called foolish and hypocrite.

7. But, O Arjuna! He who starts Karma Yoga by controlling the senses with the help of the mind and performing action without any attachment is the best.

8. You must perform your assigned duty. It is better to do work than not to do it. Without work your body cannot even survive.

9. Any action other than that which is done for the sake of sacrifice (i.e. for the sake of God = for the welfare of others) results in bondage in this world. Therefore, O Kaunteya! You do the sacrificial work without attachment.

10. After creating the people with yajna (charity), Prajapati (Brahma, the creator of the universe) said - May you grow more and more through yajna. May it give you the desired results. (from which one gets liberation)

11. Being pleased by the yagyas, the gods will please you too, and in this way, by co-operation, ultimate welfare will be achieved.

12. The gods satisfied by the yajna will give you the desired offerings. Anyone who enjoys what they have given him without repaying them is definitely a thief.

13. Those who eat the remains of a yajna are freed from all sins. Those who cook only for themselves, eat sin.

14. All living beings are born from food, and food is produced from rain. Rain occurs due to yajna, and yajna is produced by prescribed deeds.

15. Karma arises from Prakriti, Prakriti arises from Akshar-Brahma. In this way the omnipresent Brahma is always present in the yajna.

16. He who does not follow the established cycle thus mentioned certainly leads a sinful life. O Parth! Such a person lives in vain only to satisfy his senses.

17. But a man who loves his own soul, is contented and satisfied in his own soul, is not obliged to perform any duty.

18. For a self-realized person, there remains no compulsion in this world to perform his

prescribed duties, nor is there any reason for not doing such duties. He also has no personal interest in all living beings.

19. Therefore, without getting attached to the results of action, a man should continuously perform his work considering it his duty because by doing work without attachment, he attains the ultimate state.

20. Janaka and other wise men attained success by performing their prescribed duties. It is also appropriate for you to perform your duties with a view to serving the people for folk collection.

21. Whatever conduct great men follow, ordinary people imitate it. People follow the ideals they set through their exemplary actions.

22. O Partha! I have no duty in all three worlds. It is not so that I have not got anything worth getting, still I keep on doing my work.

23. If I do not perform the prescribed duties carefully, O Partha! People will follow my behavior in every way.

24. If I do not perform the prescribed duties, all these people will become corrupt. Then I will become the cause of chaos and thus the killer of all beings (in the world).

25. O Bharata! Just as ignorant people act with attachment to the results of their actions, similarly learned people should perform their duties without any attachment and with the desire to benefit the people for folk collection.

26. A wise man should not create confusion in the minds of ignorant people who perform actions with attachment to the results, but should engage them in all actions while performing his duty with detachment himself. (So that there is gradual development of God's knowledge in them)

27. All actions are performed by the modes of nature. A man fascinated by ego believes that 'I am the doer'.

28. O mighty-armed one! A person who knows the secret of the division of qualities and actions does not get attached to them, believing that 'qualities are acting in qualities'.

29. Fascinated by the qualities of nature, men remain attached to the actions of the qualities. The wise people should not destabilize those ignorant and dim-witted people.

30. Surrender all your actions to Me, abandoning attachment to the results of your actions, imbued with the knowledge of the Lord,

without any hope of gain, without any claim to ownership and abandoning laziness, fight.

31. Those men who continue to perform their duties in accordance with my advice and follow this advice faithfully and without any jealousy, are freed from the bondage of karma.

32. But those who, out of jealousy, neglect these precepts and do not follow them are to be considered as bewildered, devoid of all knowledge, and ruined in their efforts to attain perfection.

33. The wise man also acts according to his nature, because all beings follow their nature derived from the three Gunas. What good can come from repression?

34. The senses always have likes and dislikes towards their respective objects. One should not give in to them as they are obstacles in the path of self-realisation.

35. It is better to perform one's own duties faultily than to perform others' duties well. It is better to die while performing one's own duties than to engage in someone else's duties, because following someone else's path is fearful.

36. Arjuna said: O Krishna of the Vrishni dynasty! Why is a man inspired to commit sinful acts

even without wanting to? It feels like he's being forced into it.

37. Shri Bhagwan said- O Arjuna! The cause of this is the desire that arises from the interaction of Rajoguna, leading to the development of anger. This is a great sin. Consider it the enemy in this world.

38. Just as a fire is covered by smoke, a mirror by dust or the womb by its membrane, similarly knowledge is covered by the enemy in the form of lust.

39. O son of Kunti! This fire of lust which can never be satisfied is an eternal enemy. It covers the knowledge of even a wise man.

40. The senses, the mind and the intellect are the abode of this lust. Through these, this lust covers up the real knowledge of the soul and fascinates it.

    The influence of the fire of lust slows down the sharpness of intelligence, which destroys knowledge.

41. Therefore, O best of the descendants of Bharata! Suppress this sinful lust which destroys knowledge and experience, by keeping the senses under control at the very outset.

42. The organs of action are superior to material objects, the mind is superior to the senses, the intellect is higher than the mind and the soul is superior to the intellect.

43. Thus, having recognised the Self which is beyond the intellect and having controlled the mind by the Self, O mighty-armed one! Destroy this formidable enemy in the form of lust.

4. Jnanakarmasanyasa Yoga

1. Shri Bhagwan said - I preached this immortal Yoga Vidya to the Sun Deity. He spoke to Manu, the father of humans, and Manu spoke to King Ikshvaku.

2. O Arjun! In this way, this great knowledge of Yoga, known to the princely sages through tradition, was destroyed by the effect of long time.

3. Today I have told you the same ancient yogic knowledge. Because you are my devotee and friend, and this Yoga is a matter of divine secret.

4. Arjun said – You have been born just now, Sun Deity has already been born. Then how do I understand that you taught him this Yoga Vidya in the beginning.

When we are prohibited from asking questions that arise in our mind, it hinders the development of our intellect, we are unable to think of good and constructive things and demonic tendencies increase, which ultimately leads to the destruction of society.

5. Sri Bhagavan said - O Parantapa! You and I have been born many times. I remember them all, but you don't.

6. I am unborn and imperishable, and besides this I am the Lord of all beings; yet in each age, due to My nature, by the power of Maya I keep taking birth in the natural form.

7. O son of the Earth! Whenever Dharma (righteousness) weakens and the influence of Adharma (unrighteousness) increases, then I create myself.

8. I appear in every era to help the virtuous, punish the wicked, and restore goodness in society.

God is present in everyone and whenever there is any loss of path of righteousness, when we are unable to perform our duties or when we understand, we leave our ego and take refuge in God, then only goodness and God remain. And then the duty that is performed is done by the will of the Supreme Lord Shri Bhagwan or through Him. If this situation persists till the end then it is said that God was created to protect the path of rightness and promote righteousness in society.

In this manner, by giving up one's ego, 'Aham Brahmasmi' is a matter to be understood, not to be chanted.

9. O Arjun! Thus, he who knows the secret of My appearance and transcendental deeds does not take rebirth after giving up his body but attains My form.

10. Freed from attachment, fear and anger, by being absorbed in Me and by taking refuge in Me, many, purified by the austerity of knowledge, have attained My form.

11. I give fruits to those who take shelter in me in whatever manner. Whichever way it may be, O Partha! Human beings follow my path and live under my rule.

As long as a person is alive, his hands and legs are moving, so why not indulge in duty in a constructive direction in society? A person gets the results as per his actions. Everyone gets results according to his ability and actions. There is no exception to this rule in God's house (in the world).

12. Those who desire the accomplishment of momentary duties worship the deities (power in the form of parts of the Supreme Being) in this world. Through this, they get the fruits of their duties.

13. According to qualities and actions I have created four varnas (castes). Even though I am their doer, you should consider me as immortal and non-doer.

   Srimad Bhagavad Gita is the best and most accepted book. Therefore, this is the parable and the main basis for understanding the Manusmriti and other texts.

   Classification of caste was considered on the basis of its own qualities. Errors creep into any rule or thing over a period of time. Now on the basis of those errors, if someone behaves in the society on the basis of the clan in which he was born then such people do not get the wisdom to attain the highest destination. Because their mind is influenced by flawed thinking. If one wants to attain the highest ultimate destination, he must completely remove the caste-based surname acquired on the basis of birth in a clan to eliminate the influence of wrong thinking on his mind. In today's time, there are many types of duties in society based on nature and its own qualities, in such a situation they can use a surname related to their current duty.

14. I am not touched by karma, and I do not desire their fruits. Thus, those who know me well do not get bound by karma.

15. In ancient times, all the liberated souls performed their duties after knowing My divine nature, so you must follow in their footsteps and perform your duties.

16. Even intelligent people get confused in determining what is action and what is inaction. In the following manner, I shall tell you what karma is, and by knowing this you shall be free from all evils.

17. The difference between karma, prohibited karma and akarma should be understood. The pace of karma is profound.

18. Those who see inaction in action and action in inaction are wise among humans. He remains in the state of a desireless yogi even while performing all his duties.

19. He whose start of all duties are devoid of desire and resolution, and whose desire for the fruit of his actions has been burnt to ashes

by the fire of knowledge is called a Pandit by the wise.

20. He who, having renounced all desire for the fruits of his actions, remains ever satisfied and independent, even while performing all his duties (may be said to) do nothing.

21. He who is without hope, whose mind is under his control, who has renounced the feeling of accumulation and ownership of his wealth, and who acts only to keep the body functioning, is not guilty of doing his actions even while performing them.

22. He who is satisfied with the gains that come his way, who is free from the dualities of pleasure and pain, who has become free from animosity, who remains steady in both success and failure, does not get bound even while performing action.

23. He who is free from attachments, whose mind is completely stable in knowledge and who performs his actions as a sacrifice, all his actions get completely dissolved in God.

   All the duties of a wise man are for God.

24. For him the act of offering his duty is also God, the object to be offered is also God and the one

who offers the oblation of his duty in the fire of Brahma is also God. In this way, the one who has reconciled God with his duty attains the state of God in human form.

25. Some Yogis worship (perform duty for) the deities thoroughly through various kinds of oblations, while other Yogis offer oblations (duty for) the deities by offering oblations to the fire of the Supreme Brahm.

26. Some people offer their senses, such as hearing, etc., as an offering to the fire of self-control; others offer their sense objects, such as speech, etc., as an offering to the fire of self-control.

27. And many surrender all their sensory activities and vital activities to the fire of self-control ignited by the lamp of knowledge.

28. Some persons give material possessions for the oblation, some are ascetics. There are many people who practice Ashtanga Yoga. Some do self-study and Knowledge oblation. All of them are diligent Yagya performers (those who try to perform in the direction of their duties), observing difficult vows.

29. There are other people also who engage in pranayama. They practice remaining in

samadhi by stopping prana in apana and apana in prana.

-> Prana and Apana are referred to as incoming and outgoing breath.

30. There are others who, by moderation of food, sacrifice life-breathing to life-breathing. All those who perform these yajnas understand the meaning of yajnas and their sins are destroyed by the yajna.

31. Those who consume the nectar-like food obtained by performing yajnas attain the state of the eternal Brahma. O Kurus! If a person who does not perform yajnas cannot survive in this world, then how can he achieve the state of Brahma in the afterlife?

32. In this way, various kinds of Yajnas (methods of performing one's duty) have been described in the Veda. By understanding the methods of duty in this way, you will attain salvation.

33. O Paratamp! Knowledge-yajna is better than material-yajna, because, O Partha! Only through knowledge can duty reach its pinnacle.

34. You should learn this by serving the wise men who know the truth and by asking them questions humbly and with discretion again

and again. They will satisfy you with that knowledge.

35. After attaining that knowledge you will never have such attachment again. Through this knowledge, you will be able to see that all living beings are parts of Me, the Supreme Being.

36. Even if you are considered the most sinful of all sinners, you will completely cross the ocean of sorrow by boarding the boat of divine knowledge.

37. O Arjun! Just as a fire turns its fuel into ashes when it burns, similarly the fire of knowledge turns all the deeds into ashes.

Doing one's duty may be painful for others and may be a sin, but it is Dharma if the duty is done with the spirit of non-violence and service in the form of renouncing the consequences - doing one's duty in this manner does not incur sin.

38. There is nothing as sacred in this world as good knowledge. A person engaged in spiritual warfare (a person immersed in duty) who is adept in yoga, keeps getting knowledge within himself whenever the need arises.

39. He who has faith in God, who is eager to acquire knowledge and who has controlled his senses, attains knowledge and after attaining knowledge, he immediately finds supreme peace.

40. He who, due to ignorance, is doubtful and faithless towards God, gets destroyed. For one who is doubtful about God, there is no happiness either in this life or after life.

41. O Dhananjaya! He who has renounced the desire for the results of his actions through the yoga of equanimity and has dispelled his doubts through knowledge, for such a self-realized person, actions are not bondage.

42. Therefore, O Bharata! Destroy the doubts in your heart regarding God which have arisen out of ignorance with the sword of self-knowledge and stand up with equanimity in your mind.

5. Karma Sanyasa Yoga

1. Arjun said- O Krishna! First, you ask us to renounce action, then you ask us to perform our duties with devotion. Please tell me with certainty which of these two is better?

   Having full faith in God, one will perform the duty in a good way while searching for the right way and only then will one know that the best way is to perform the duty by renouncing the desire for the fruit of the action.

   If you don't even try, how will you know what the right way is? God does good to only those who do good to themselves with good intentions.

2. Shri Bhagwan said -

   Renunciation of actions and efforts for duties both lead to salvation. Among them also, efforts for duties (Karma yoga) are better than the renunciation of actions (Karma Sanyas).

I have given up doing my duties - when such a feeling comes, the person becomes free and comfortable and then he should make efforts to fulfil his duties. As long as a person is alive, his hands and legs will move. So the good and constructive thing would be to strive to perform our duties in a good manner.

3. O mighty-armed one!

The man who neither hates the results of actions nor desires them is a continual ascetic, free from all dilemmas and is easily and happily free from the bondages of karma.

4. Those with limited knowledge say that Sankhya, that is, analytical knowledge, and Karma yoga are two different things. Pandit i.e. wise person says that one who stays well established in any one of these gets the benefits of both.

5. The place which a Sankhya Marg follower gets, the same place is also got by a Karmayogi. He who sees Sankhya knowledge and Karma Yoga as one and the same is the true seer.

6. O mighty-armed one! Without Karma Yoga, the renunciation of action is painful, but a sage who maintains equanimity in his mind soon attains salvation.

Muni = a good person with deep thought in his mind

7. He who has practised yoga for the sake of duty, who has purified his heart, who has conquered his mind and senses, and who considers all creatures as his own, such a man does not remain involved in his duty even while performing it.

8. The man who has understood God and who understands the Truth, knows that while seeing, hearing, touching, smelling, tasting, walking, sleeping and breathing, he is not actually doing anything.

9. While speaking, while excreting, while opening and closing the eyes, one understands that only the senses are engaged in their respective objects.

10. The person who surrenders the fruits of his actions to God and performs his duties without attachment (giving up desire for the fruits of his actions), remains unaffected by sinful acts just as water cannot touch the leaf of a lotus flower.

11. Yogis give up attachment to the body, mind, intellect or even to the senses and perform their duties to purify the soul.

12. The soul engaged in Yoga gives up attachment to the fruits of action and attains supreme peace, but those whose souls are not absorbed in the Supreme Lord are driven by desire and have attachment to the fruits of their actions and hence remain in bondage.

13. When the soul in an embodied body controls its nature and gives up the idea of performing all actions from its mind, then it lives happily in the physical body which is like a city with nine gates, without doing or getting anything done.

14. The Lord of the world neither creates doership nor action nor does He coordinate action with its result. Nature does everything.

15. God is not responsible for anyone's sins or virtues. Due to knowledge being covered by ignorance from all sides, a person becomes confused about what to do.

16. But for those whose ignorance is destroyed by knowledge, knowledge illuminates the soul like the sun.

17. Those whose sins have been washed away by knowledge, those who meditate on God, are absorbed in Him, remain steadfast in Him, and consider Him as everything, attain salvation.

18. Due to their Sattvik knowledge, wise men look at a learned and courteous Brahmin, a cow, an elephant, a dog and a dog-eater with the same vision.

19. Those whose mind is stable in equanimity have conquered the world while still in this body. He is as blameless as Brahma and always remains situated in Brahma.

20. He who neither rejoices on getting a pleasant thing nor is perturbed on getting an unpleasant thing, who is of steady mind, who is free from attachment and who knows Brahma, remains situated in Brahma.

    Just like there is the whole universe outside; similarly when the soul becomes absorbed in it, is a similar entity in the whole universe.

21. He who is not attached to sense pleasures lives happily in his heart. A person who has devoted himself in union with God, experiences everlasting happiness.

22. O son of Kunti! The pleasure obtained from physical senses does not last forever; it has a definite beginning and end. After the end of such momentary happiness there is sorrow. Therefore, the wise man does not take pleasure in it.

23. The man who has attained the power to bear the force of his desire and anger before giving up his body, is a yogi, is happy.

24. The one who feels happiness in his heart, who has peace in his heart, who has got intuition, that Yogi who is in the form of Brahma, attains the ultimate bliss of God.

25. Those whose sins have been destroyed, whose doubts have been subdued, whose minds are absorbed in Self-realization and who delight in doing good to all beings, attain the supreme bliss of God.

26. The ascetic souls who have freed themselves from desire and anger, who have subdued their minds and who have attained Self-realisation are in the supreme bliss of the Supreme Being.

27-28. By rejecting external pleasures, by fixing the gaze between the eyebrows, by equalizing the speed of the incoming and outgoing breaths of the nose, by controlling the senses, mind and intellect, the sage, who is determined to attain liberation and is devoid of desire, fear and anger, remains ever free.

29. That sage, knowing that I (the Supreme Lord) am the ultimate enjoyer of all yajnas and austerities and that I am the Lord of all the worlds and deities and the benefactor and well-wisher of all living beings, attains peace.

6. Dhyana Yoga (Meditation)

1. Shri Bhagwan said -

   A person who does his duty without any desire for the fruit of his actions is a Sanyasi, a Yogi. Not he who, in order to become a Yogi, stops having the intense desire (in the form of fire) within himself and does not perform any duty.

2. O Pandava! What is called Sannyasa, you should consider it as Yoga, because one who has not given up the resolutions of the mind can never become a Yogi.

3. For the sage who wants to be a yogi (dutiful), his duty is the means; for one who has mastered yoga, peace is the means.

4. When a man is not attached to the objects of the senses or to action and renounces all resolutions, then he is said to have attained Yoga.

5. Man must save his soul with his mind and not let it fall. This mind is both man's friend and enemy.

6. Only he who has conquered his mind with his understanding has a soul friend. He who has not conquered his mind, treats himself like an enemy.

7. He who has conquered his mind is steadfast in devotion to God because he has attained peace; he remains the same in cold and heat, in pleasure and pain, in honour and dishonour.

8. One who is satisfied with knowledge and experience, who is unshakable, who has conquered his senses and to whom clay, stone and gold are the same, such a man established in spiritual knowledge is called a Yogi.

9. The one who has equal feelings towards well-wishers, friends, enemies, neutrals, mediators, jealous people, enemies, relatives, saints and sinners is the best.

10. The yogi should sit alone in solitude, carefully controlling his mind, being free from all desires, abandoning the feeling of collecting anything and focusing his mind on God.

11-12. For the practice of Dhyana Yoga, the Yogi should spread a soft, padded cloth for sitting in a solitary and sacred place. The place should neither be too high nor too low. Sitting there on that seat, controlling one's mind and senses, practicing meditation to purify one's soul.

13-14. Keeping one's body, neck and head straight and steady, not looking here and there, fixing one's gaze between one's eyebrows, be in perfect peace, be fearless, remain firm in celibacy, subdue one's mind, concentrate on Me and make Me one's ultimate goal.

15. Thus the Yogi whose mind is controlled and whose soul is united with the Supreme Being, after giving up the body attains the abode of God. That is, on attaining my state one achieves the ultimate peace in the form of salvation.

16. O Arjun! This yoga is not for someone who eats too much or eats too little or who sleeps too much or does not sleep enough.

17. By practicing Yoga, an individual who moderates their consumption of food and in recreation, fulfills their responsibilities, and maintains a regular sleep schedule can eliminate his every sorrow.

18. When the mind becomes free from all desires and becomes disciplined and becomes stable only in its own soul, then the person is called a Yogi.

19. The condition of a yogi with a steady mind who is trying to unite his soul with the Supreme Being is said to be like a lamp remaining motionless in an airless place.

20. The mind controlled by the practice of Yoga becomes tranquil, and by recognising the soul by the soul, it becomes satisfied within its own soul.

21. One experiences the supreme bliss that is beyond the senses and comprehended by the intellect, and being established in this Yoga one does not deviate from the essential truth.

22. In this Yoga a happy man does not consider any other benefit greater than this and is not perturbed even by the greatest difficulties.

23. The state free from all sorrows should be understood as the state of Yoga, and it can be achieved with determination and without getting bored.

24. Having completely renounced all desires which arise from the resolution, and having controlled all the senses with the mind,

25. With a steady mind, the yogi gradually becomes calm and concentrates his mind on the Self and does not think of anything else.

26. Wherever the fickle and unstable mind runs, the yogi should pull it back from there and bring it under his control.

27. The sinless Yogi, whose mind is well-pacified, whose desires arising from the mode of passion (Rajoguna) have been subdued, and who has become one with the Supreme Being, attains the highest happiness.

28. Thus, the self-controlled yogi constantly engaged in the practice of Yoga becomes free from all sins and experiences perfect bliss by worshipping the Supreme Being.

29. The Yogi who is equanimous everywhere sees Me in all beings and all beings in Me.

30. He who sees me everywhere and sees everything in me, is never out of my sight and I am never invisible to his sight.

31. The Yogi who is absorbed in Me and worships Me, knowing Me to be present in all beings, remains in Me while performing his duties in the external life.

32. O Arjun! The person who keeps his mind balanced even in happiness and sorrow and behaves well with everyone is a great Yogi.

33. Arjun said – O Madhusudan Lord Krishna! Due to the fickleness of my mind, I am unable to see

the stability of the Yoga of equality that you described.

34. O Krishna! The mind is very fickle, distracting, strong and stubborn. I think that controlling it is as difficult as controlling the wind.

35. Sri Bhagavan said- O mighty-armed one! No doubt it is difficult to control the fickle mind, yet, O son of Kunti! It can be controlled by constant practice and detachment.

36. It is my opinion that it is very difficult for a person whose mind is not under his control to practice yoga; a person whose mind is under his control and who takes appropriate measures can practice yoga.

37. Arjun said- O Lord Shri Krishna! What is the condition of one who has devotion but cannot control himself due to his fickle mind and so due to imperfection he is unable to succeed in Yoga?

38. O mighty-armed Lord Krishna! Doesn't a man who has deviated from the practice of Yoga and strayed from the path of Brahm, losing both spiritual and material success, ultimately perish like scattered clouds, with no place left for him in any realm?

39. O Lord Krishna! This is my doubt and I request you to remove it completely. No one else except you can remove this doubt.

40. The Lord said: O Partha! Such people perish neither in this world nor in the afterworld. O dear friend! The person who does good deeds never faces misfortune.

41. A man who deviates from the path of Yoga attains the place reserved for the virtuous and, after staying there for a long time, is born in the home of a man of means.

42. Or (if he became corrupt in the way of yoga) he is born in the family of a knowledgeable Yogi. Such a birth is certainly rare in this world.

43. O son of Kuru Arjuna! On taking such a birth, he again receives the intellect and sanskars of his previous birth and strives for perfect yoga with the objective of attaining complete success.

44. He is compelled by the practice of his previous life to become drawn towards Yoga. This curiosity for Yoga transcends the state of performing mantras etc, Vedic rituals.

45. The yogi, striving with true devotion, becomes free from sin and becomes purified through many births and attains the ultimate goal.

46. The yogi is superior to the ascetic, the wise and the performers of rituals. Therefore, O Arjun! You become a yogi.

47. Among all the yogis, I consider the one who concentrates his mind on me and worships me with devotion to be the best yogi.

7. Gyan Vigyan Yoga
(Godly Knowledge)

1. Shri Bhagwan said -

   O Parth! Now listen, how you can recognize me definitely and completely by concentrating your mind on Me and practising Yoga taking shelter in Me.

2. I will tell you this experiential knowledge in full. After knowing this, there will be nothing more left to know in this world.

3. Out of thousands of people who strive to achieve perfection in Yoga, only a few attain perfection and out of them a few know me truly.

4. My nature is divided into these eight types: earth, water, fire, air, sky, mind, intellect and ego.

5. This is my unconscious (inanimate) nature. Oh mighty-armed Arjuna! My other nature, which is superior to these, is the living form by which this universe is sustained.

6. You should understand these two natures as the reason for the origin of all living beings. I am the cause of the origin and destruction of all inanimate and living beings.

7. O Dhananjaya! There is no other truth greater than mine. Whatever exists in this world is dependent on me, just like pearls are strung on a thread.

   Dhananjaya = Arjuna who conquered wealth

8. O Arjuna, son of Kunti! I am the essence in water, I am the brightness in the Sun and the Moon, I am the sacred syllable Om in all the Vedas, I am the sound of the sky, and I am the strength within humans.

9. I am the fragrance of the earth's soil, I am the heat of the fire. I am the life of all living beings and I am the penance of all ascetics.

10. O Partha! Consider me the eternal (from beginning to end) seed of all living beings. I am the wisdom of the wise, I am the brilliance of the brilliant.

11. I am strength of the strong being without passion and attachment; and O best of the Bharatas! I am the passion in accordance with Dharma in all beings.

12. All these Satvik, Rajasik and Tamasic sentiments, consider that they have originated from me only. I am not subject to them, but they are subject to me.

13. Because the whole world is fascinated by these three mode feelings, it is unable to recognize the imperishable Supreme Lord who is above and distinct from them.

14. It is difficult to overcome My divine Maya (illusion) which consists of the three modes of nature, but those who surrender to Me alone, easily overcome this Maya.

15. Those who do evil deeds, who are foolish, who are lowly among men, whose intellect has been misled by delusion and who possess the atheistic nature of the demons, such wicked ones do not take refuge in Me.

16. O best of the Bharatas! Four types of virtuous people worship me - the unhappy, the curious, those wishing to attain something and the knowledgeable.

17. Of all these the wise man, who is always devoted to the One Brahm with steadfast equanimity, is the best. I am very dear to the wise and the wise are dear to me.

18. Though all these devotees are good, the wise man who has attained My knowledge is Me Himself, because he devotes himself entirely to Yoga, takes My refuges and worships Me, knowing that there is no better goal than attaining Me.

19. After many births, the wise man, who understands that all that exists is Vasudeva (Godly) - finds Me. A Mahatma who understands like this is very rare.

20. Those whose knowledge has been carried away by many material desires, take refuge in other deities by resorting to different methods of worship according to their nature.

21. I am present in every living being in the form of God. Whichever devotee wishes to worship other deities with devotion, I strengthen his faith in each form.

22. He worships each form of Me with devotion and through them gets fulfilled all his desires made by Me.

23. The fruits that those with little intelligence receive are perishable. Those who worship deities find deities, those who worship me find Me.

24. I am not understandable to the senses of humans. Foolish men, who do not know My absolutely indestructible, supreme and incomparable form, consider Me to be something that can be perceived by their senses.

25. I am never revealed to the foolish and the ignorant. For them I remain covered by my Yogamaya, so they are unable to know that I am unborn and indestructible.

26. O Arjun! I know all the beings who have existed in the past, those who exist now and those who will exist in the future but no one knows Me.

27. O Bharatavanshi! O conqueror of enemies! After being born in this world, all creatures are afflicted with attachment to the duality of happiness and sorrow, which arise out of desire and hatred.

28. But those virtuous souls whose sins have been destroyed by their good intentions and pious deeds, become free from the attachment to the dualities of happiness and sorrow and worship me with determination.

29. Those who take refuge in me and strive to be free from old age and death, know the complete Brahm, spirituality and duty completely.

    Atmani adhi iti adhyatma: = concentrating the mind in the soul is called adhyatma.

30. Those who know Me as the Supreme Lord, the Ruler of the entire material universe and of all deities and the controller of all yajnas, remain in equanimity with their minds focussed on yoga and remain fixed in devotion to Me even at the time of death.

8. Akshara Brahma Yoga (Attainment of the Lord)

(Bhakti Yoga towards the Indestructible Eternal God)

In this chapter the sequence of a person's development in understanding God is explained.

1. Arjuna said: O Purushottama Lord Krishna! What is the nature of this Brahma? What is spirituality? What is Karma? What is called Adhibhut? And what is called Adhidaiv (supreme god)?

2. O Madhusudan (Shri Krishna)! What is Adhiyajna in this body and what is it like? And how can one who has subjugated himself recognize you at the time of death?

3. Shri Bhagwan said- The best immortal thing is Brahma. Brahma always resides in every living being by its nature and that is spirituality. The

activity of creation that produces the physical body of living beings is called karma.

4. Adhibhuta is my perishable form. Adhidaiwat is my living form residing in it. And O best of men, Arjuna! I am the ultimate ruler of the supreme yajna, purified by the yajna that resides within this body.

5. There is no doubt that at the end of his life, he who gives up his body while remembering me attains my form.

6. O Arjuna, son of Kunti! Whatever form a man remembers at the last moment while leaving his body, he attains that state by remaining always absorbed in its meditation.

7. Therefore, always worship Me and fight within yourself for yoga for duty; thus, by fixing your mind and intellect on Me, you will certainly find Me.

8. O Partha! A person who practices Yoga with his mind and intellect with unwavering devotion and remembers the Supreme God, certainly attains that divine Supreme Being.

9. The person who always meditates on the divine Supreme Being who is omniscient, ancient, the one who keeps the system in order, the subtlest

of all, the protector of all, unimaginable, and shines like the sun beyond the darkness of ignorance

10. And who at the last moment of his life stabilizes his mind with the power of devotion and yoga and firmly establishes his life force between the eyebrows, he attains that divine Supreme Being Shri Bhagwan.

11. I will provide a short overview of the path leading to immortality as described in the Vedas, where sages enter the Brahma without attachment, and those who practice celibacy can achieve the desired attainment.

12. By controlling all the sense gates of the body, by fixing the mind in the heart, and the life-force in the brain, by concentrating through Yoga;

13. The person who gives up his body while chanting the one-syllable Brahma ॐ and remembering me, attains the highest position (ultimate salvation).

14. O Partha! The yogi who constantly remembers me with an unwavering mind and is always focused on me attains me easily.

15. The great soul who has attained the ultimate salvation to God is not reborn in this temporary

world full of sorrows because he has attained the ultimate success.

16. O Arjuna, son of Kunti! From Brahma's realm downwards, all the realms are such from which one has to return for rebirth. But after reaching me no one is reborn again.

17. One day of Brahma for a thousand Yugas and one night of Brahma for a thousand Yugas, those who know this understand the day and night (i.e. time in the universe).

18. When the day of Brahma begins, all beings emerge from the unmanifested state, and when the night comes, they are destroyed, and they all again merge into the unmanifested state.

19. O Partha! Whenever the day of Brahma comes, these groups of beings are born in this manner, and as soon as the night of Brahma arrives, they become helpless and disappear into the unmanifested state.

20. But besides this unmanifested state, there is the supremely eternal unmanifested existence which is not destroyed even when all living beings are destroyed.

21. This state of being unmanifested is considered imperishable and is the final destination where there is no rebirth - it is where I ultimately reside.

22. O Partha! Sri Bhagavan is the most great, omnipresent, everything resides in Him. He can be attained by exclusive devotion.

23. O Greatest of Bharatas! Now I will tell you about the different periods in which the Yogi attains salvation or rebirth after giving up his body from this world.

24. Those who are knowledgeable of the Supreme Brahma, attain that Supreme Brahma by abandoning their body in this world during the six months of Uttarayan, in the Shukla Paksh, during the day when the flames of the fire are rising.

25. Those who give up their body during the six months of Dakshinayana, in the dark fortnight, when smoke is spread, reach the Moon world and are reborn.

    People who engage in acts of selfless service, possess knowledge of the Supreme Lord, and live in the light of wisdom, ultimately achieve salvation and are freed from the cycle of reincarnation. And those who live in the darkness of ignorance are reborn. Until one attains knowledge and gets liberation, rebirth continues.

26. In the world, the two traditional paths of the light of knowledge and the darkness of

ignorance have been understood. Through the path of knowledge man attains salvation and through the path of ignorance he gets rebirth.

27. O Partha! A yogi who understands both these paths does not fall into attachment. Therefore, O Arjun! You should always remain stable in Yoga.

28. Having known all this, the Yogi reaches a supreme state beyond the fruits obtained by the study of the Vedas, performing yajnas, austerities and charity, and attains the Supreme Abode.

9. Rajavidya Rajaguhya Yoga

1. Lord Shri Krishna said-

   Since you are not hating anyone, I will give you very deep knowledge based on experience, after understanding which you will be freed from rebirth in this painful world.

2. This most secret knowledge is the best of all knowledge; it is sacred, excellent and gives direct experience. It is in accordance with Dharma, it is easy to practice, and it is indestructible.

3. O Parantapa (Arjuna who has controlled the disorders of the senses through penance)! Those who do not have faith in this Sanatan Dharma do not attain me (God). In such a situation, they return to this physical world again and again in the cycle of birth and death.

4. This entire universe is pervaded by My unmanifested power. All living beings are situated in me, but I am not situated in them.

5. Nevertheless, the entire creation that I have produced remains in Me. Just look at the glory of my yoga. Although I am the sustainer of all living beings and am omnipresent, I am not a part of this visible world. Because I am the cause of their origin.

6. Just as the omnipresent air is eternally present in the sky, similarly the entire creation exists in the omnipresent God.

7. O Arjuna, son of Kunti! At the end of a Kalpa the entire creation merges into My nature and at the beginning of another Kalpa I create them again.

8. With my Maya, I repeatedly create all the living beings that are under the influence of nature.

9. O conqueror of wealth (Dhananjaya) Arjuna! These actions do not bind Me, because I am always indifferent and free from attachment towards them.

10. O son of Kunti! Under my authority nature produces all movable and immovable creatures. Under its influence the world is created and destroyed again and again.

11. Ignorant people do not know My (the omnipresent God's) divine nature within the body and keep ridiculing Me.

12. They are attracted to demonic and devilish thoughts that keep them infatuated. Their hopes remain in vain, their actions remain in vain and hence their knowledge remains in vain.

13. O Partha! People with great souls take shelter of the divine nature and worship Me with perfect faith, knowing Me to be the immortal Lord among all beings.

14. These great souls, constantly singing My glories, striving with firm resolve, salute Me with devotion and worship Me while always engaged in Yoga.

15. Others worship me by the yajna of knowledge. They worship Me with one form, with many forms, and in the cosmic form facing all directions.

16. I am the ritual, I am the yajna, I am the Pindadaan given to the ancestors, the herbs for the yajna (Havan samagri), the divine sound (mantra), ghee, fire and the offering.

17. I am the father of this universe, I am the mother, I am the shelter, I am the grandfather, I am the one to be known, I am the holy sound ॐ, as well as the Rigveda, Samaveda and Yajurveda.

18. I am the goal, the protector, the master, the witness, the refuge and the well-wishing friend. I am the foundation, shelter and the indestructible seed of everything in creation and destruction.

19. I bring the heat, I am the one who stops the rain and lets it pour. I am immortality and I am also death. O Arjun! I am the true soul and also a perishable matter.

20. Those who understand the three Vedas remain free from sins by drinking the nectar of God's knowledge and while performing their duties with devotion to Me, they pray for heaven, having attained which they enjoy heaven which is a state of happiness.

21. Thus, after enjoying that vast heavenly world, when their merits are exhausted, they again return to the mortal world; thus, those who perform actions according to the Vedas for sense-pleasure with a desire for their fruits are engaged in the cycle of birth and death.

22. But I bear the burden of Yoga (attainment of the unobtained) and Kshema (protection of the attainment of what has been obtained) of those who worship me with exclusive devotion, always thinking of Me.

23. O son of Kunti! Those who devoutly worship other deities, even if they do so erroneously, are actually worshiping Me.

24. I am the Lord who enjoys all yajnas. Those who do not recognize this true form of mine, fall down.

25. Those who worship deities attain deity's place, those who worship ancestors attain the world of ancestors, those who worship ghosts and spirits attain their worlds and those who worship me attain my highest world.

26. If someone offers me a leaf, a flower, a fruit or water with a pure heart and love and devotion, I definitely accept it.

    God residing in living beings accepts gifts offered to Him with a pure heart.

27. Therefore, O son of Kunti! Whatever you do, whatever you eat, whatever you offer or donate, and whatever penance you perform, do it as a gift given to me.

28. In this way you will be freed from the bondage of karma which gives good and bad results and, having attained equanimity of renunciation of results, you will be freed from the cycle of birth and death and will find Me.

29. I live with equanimity towards all living beings. I don't have anyone dear or unloved. All those who worship me with devotion are in me and I am in them.

30. If even the most wicked person worships me with exclusive devotion, he should be considered a saint. Because now he has a good resolve.

31. He immediately becomes righteous and attains everlasting peace. O son of Kunti! You can know for sure that my devotee never perishes.

32. O Partha! Whoever takes refuge in me, whether they are born in a low family, or are women, Vaishyas or Shudras, they too attain the highest goal, salvation.

33. Then what to say about the holy Brahmins and the devout Rajrishis. Therefore, coming to this temporary, sorrowful world, you should worship me with devotion.

   Brahmin = true expert in the knowledge of Brahma and Dharma

   Rishi = seer of the real truth

   Srimad Bhagavad Gita is the best and most accepted book. Therefore, this is the parable and basis for understanding the Manusmriti and other texts.

Chapter 4, Divine Saying 13 – Classification of castes was considered on the basis of nature and its own qualities. Errors creep into any rule or thing over a period of time. Now on the basis of those errors, if someone behaves in the society on the basis of the family/clan in which he was born then such people do not get the wisdom to attain the highest, ultimate destination. Because their mind is influenced by flawed thinking. If one wants to attain the highest ultimate destination, he must completely remove the caste-based surname acquired on the basis of birth in a clan to eliminate the influence of wrong thinking on his mind. In today's time, there are many types of duties in society based on nature and its own qualities, in such a situation they can use a surname related to their work.

Both men and women are precious. Both in the world and in the body complement each other.

34. Fix your mind on me, be my devotee, worship me, bow to me. In this way, by keeping yourself disciplined and making me your goal, you will reach me.

10. Vibhuti Yoga

1. The Lord said: O mighty-armed Arjuna! Now, listen to my ultimate words. Since you are my dear friend, I will impart this great knowledge to you for your welfare.

2. Even the deities and the great sages do not know my origin, because I am the cause of their origin in every way.

3. The wise man who lives in the mortal world and knows me as unborn, eternal and the Lord of all the worlds, remains free from all sins.

4-5. Wisdom, knowledge, freedom from doubt and delusion, forgiveness, truth, self-control and peace, happiness and sorrow, birth and death, fear and fearlessness, non-violence, equanimity of mind, contentment, austerity, charity, fame and infamy – these various qualities of living beings are produced by me alone.

6. The Saptarishis, the four Maharishis before them and Manu, all originated from my mind and from them, all the living beings residing in the various worlds originated.

7. He who completely knows my glory and yogic power remains devoted to me through unshakable yoga. There is no doubt about this.

8. I am the cause of the origin of everything and the entire creation runs from me. Knowing this, wise people worship me with devotion.

9. The thoughts of My pure devotees become fixed on Me; their lives are totally devoted to My service and they experience supreme satisfaction and joy in imparting knowledge to one another and talking about Me.

10. To those who thus perform My sacred ritual and worship Me with love, I grant the concentration of the intellect by which they find Me.

11. Taking pity on them, I destroy the darkness of their ignorance with the luminous lamp of knowledge situated in their hearts.

12-13. Arjun said- O God! You are the Supreme Brahma, the Supreme Abode, the Supreme Holy and the Supreme Truth. All the sages, Devarshis, Narada, Asit, Deval and Vyas consider you as the immortal divine being, the original god, the unborn, and the embodiment of God, and you yourself also say the same.

14. O Keshava (Lord Krishna)! I believe what you say to be absolutely true. Neither gods nor demons know your manifested form.

15. O Supreme Being! O Father of all beings, O God of all beings, O God of all deities, O Lord of the entire universe! Only you know yourself through yourself.

16. Kindly tell me in detail about Your divine manifestations (powers) by which You exist in all these worlds.

17. Oh Supreme Yogi Shri Krishna! How do I meditate on You constantly and know You? O Supreme Lord, in what various forms should you be remembered?

18. Oh Janardana Sri Krishna! Please describe your yogic powers and glories in detail again. Because I am not getting satisfied by listening to your nectar-like words.

19. The Lord said: O Arjuna, best of the Kurus! Yes, now I will describe to you My major divinely glorious forms because there is no end to My expansion.

20. O the possessor of thick beautiful hair, Arjuna! I am the soul present in the heart of all beings. I am the beginning, middle and end of all beings or things.

21. I am Vishnu among the Adityas, I am the radiant Sun among the lights, I am Marichi among the winds, I am the Moon among the nakshatras.

22. Among the Vedas I am the Samaveda, among the deities, I am Indra, the King of Heaven, among the senses I am the mind and among living beings I am the life force consciousness.

23. I am Shankar among all the Rudras. I am Kubera, the deity of wealth among the Yakshas and demons. I am Agni among the Vasus and I am Meru among all the mountain peaks.

24. O Partha (Arjuna)! Consider me Brihaspati, the chief priest among all the priests. I am Kartikeya, the best among all commanders and I am the ocean among all water bodies.

25. Amongst the sages I am the great Bhrigu, among the voices I am the divine one syllable ॐ, among all the sacrifices I am the sacred silent Japa-yajna and among all the immovable objects I am the huge Himalayas.

26. Among all trees I am the Peepal, among divine sages I am Narada, among Gandharvas I am

Chitrarath and among Siddha sages I am Kapil Muni.

27. Among the horses, know me as Uchchaihshrava, who was born at the time of churning the ocean for nectar. Among elephants, I am the chief elephant of Indra, Airavat, and among humans, I am the good king.

28. Among weapons I am Vajra, among cows I am Kamadhenu, I am Kamadeva, the cause of creation of all subjects and among serpents I am Vasuki (who worked as a rope to tie the mountain during the churning of sea).

29. Among the nagas I am Sheshnag Ananta, among the aquatic creatures I am Varundev, among the ancestors I am Aryama, and among those who enforce rules and regulations I am Yama.

30. Among demons I am Prahlada, the king of devotees; among those who calculate I am time of death; among animals I am the lion, the king of animals; and among birds I am Garuda, the carrier of Lord Vishnu, the best.

31. Among the purifiers I am the pure air, among the weapon bearers I am Rama, among the fishes I am the best crocodile and among the rivers I am the purifying Ganga.

32. O Arjun! I am the beginning, middle and end of all creations; I am the spiritual knowledges among all knowledge and I am the decisive truth among logicians.

33. Among letters I am अ and among compounds I am the Dvandva Samasa. I am the unchangeable time of death and I am also the omnipresent Creator, whose faces are present in all directions.

34. I am the death that conquers all, and I am also the cause of the origin of all that will be born in the future. Among women, I am fame, wealth, speech, memory, intelligence, patience and forgiveness.

35. I am the Brihat Sama in the songs of the Samaveda and I am the Gayatri Mantra in the verses. Among the months I am Margashirsha and among the seasons I am the flower-blooming spring.

36. I am the deceit of gamblers; I am the brilliance of the Brilliant. I am victory, I am courage and I am the goodness of people with Satvik feelings.

37. I am Vasudeva among the Vrishni clan, I am Arjuna among the Pandavas. I am Vyasa among the sages and I am Ushana among the poets.

38. I am the punishment of the ruler who suppresses anarchy, I am the policy of those who seek victory. I am the silence in mysteries and I am the knowledge of the wise.

39. O Arjun! Not only this, I am the parent seed of the entire universe. There is no living or inanimate object that exists without me.

40. O Arjuna, conqueror of evil! There is no end to my divine powers. Whatever I have told you is merely an indication of my powers.

41. Whatever is glorious, great or influential, know that it has been created from a portion of My radiance.

42. But, O Arjuna! What do you need this vast knowledge for? I am present in this whole universe with just a part of myself.

11. Vishwaroopdarshan Yoga

1. Arjun said - You have shown mercy on me and told me this ultimate spiritual secret, after listening to which, my attachment has now been dispelled.

2. I heard from you in detail about the origin and destruction of beings. O lotus-eyed Krishna! Similarly, I also heard about your imperishable glory.

3. O Lord! You are what you say you are. O Purushottam! I wish to see that huge divine form of yours.

4. O Lord! If you consider it possible for me to have that vision then O Yogeshwar! Please show me your immortal universal form.

5. Shri Bhagwan said- O Partha (Arjuna)! You see hundreds and thousands of My forms, of various divine colors and shapes.

6. O Bharata (Arjuna)! See the Adityas, the Vasus, the Rudras, the two Ashwinikumars and the Maruts. See many more wonders that have never been seen before.

7. O Gudakesh (Arjuna)! Here you see the entire world, all living and non-living things, and whatever you want to see, see them all gathered in my body.

8. But you will not be able to see me with these human eyes of yours. Therefore, I am giving you divine sight. Now behold my divine opulence in the cosmic form.

9. Sanjaya said- O King Dhritarashtra! By saying this, Yogeshwar Lord Krishna showed his divine cosmic form to Arjuna.

10. That gigantic form had many faces and eyes; there were many wondrous sights in it. The figure was adorned with multiple divine ornaments and was holding various divine weapons.

11. He was wearing many divine garlands and clothes. And they were coated with divine fragrance and ointments. Thus, He was wonderful in every way, radiant, infinite, and spread in all directions.

12. If thousands of suns shine together in the sky, then that brightness cannot possibly be like the brightness of the Supreme God.

13. At that time, Arjuna saw the entire universe divided into various forms, situated at one place, in the cosmic form of the God of gods.

14. Then Dhananjaya (Arjuna), surprised and thrilled, his head bowed down and hands folded, started praying to God and said –

15. Arjun said- O Lord Krishna! I see all the deities and various other living entities gathered within your body. I see Lord Brahma (seated on the lotus), Lord Shiva, all the sages and divine serpents.

16. I see in Your infinite body many arms, stomachs, mouths and eyes spread everywhere. You have no end, no middle, no beginning. O God of the universe! I am seeing your cosmic form.

17. I can hardly see You, wearing the crown, mace and discus, a mass of effulgence gleaming all around, dazzling, like a fire blazing on all sides, and resounding and incomparable like the Sun.

18. You are the immortal God who is to be known. You are the eternal Purushottam, the foundation of this universe and the ultimate protector of the eternal (sanatan) human religion.

19. You have no beginning, middle or end, your power is infinite. You have innumerable arms, you have eyes like the sun and the moon, your face is like a blazing fire whose radiance is scorching the entire universe.

20. You alone occupy all the space between the sky and the earth and in all directions. O great soul! Seeing your wonderful fierce cosmic form, all the three worlds are getting frightened.

21. Here groups of deities are entering into You, and some of them are extremely frightened and with folded hands are praising You. The group of Maharishis and Siddhas are using the chant "be blessed!" to honor you with extremely praiseworthy mantras.

22. The Rudras, the Adityas, the Vasus, the Sadhyas, the Vishwadevas, the two Aśvins, the Maruts, the Pitris, the Gandharvas, the Yakshas, the Asuras and the groups of the Siddhas are all looking at You in amazement.

23. O mighty-armed one! Seeing your huge cosmic form, which appears terrifying due to its many faces, eyes, arms, thighs, legs, stomachs and dreadful teeth, all the people are troubled with fear and I too am troubled like them.

24. O omnipresent Vishnu! Beholding Your cosmic form touching the sky, glittering in many

colours, with a wide open mouth and huge gleaming eyes, my soul is filled with fear. Neither am I able to have patience nor is my mind at peace.

25. Seeing Your face, which is like the fire of death and has fearsome teeth, I have lost my way and have become restless. O Lord of the deities! O shelter of the whole world! Please be pleased with me.

26-27. The sons of Dhritarashtra, their own assistant kings, Bhishma, Drona, Karna, and our other chief warriors, too, are all heading towards Your fearsome mouth with its large teeth. Many of their heads can be seen crushed and stuck between your teeth

28. Just as many large streams of rivers rush towards the ocean, similarly these valiant warriors of the human world are entering Your fierce mouth with blazing fire.

29. Just as insects quickly rush towards a burning fire for their destruction, similarly all these people are quickly entering your terrible mouth for their destruction.

30. You are licking and swallowing all the worlds from all sides with your blazing mouth. O omnipresent Vishnu! Your fiery rays are

spreading across the entire world and scorching it with their intense heat.

31. O God of gods! Please tell me who are you in such a fierce form? I prostrate infront of you, please be pleased with me. I would like to know the primary reason you are saying this because I am unable to understand what your purpose is.

32. Shri Bhagwan said: I am the expanded time of death, the destroyer of the worlds. I have come here to destroy the worlds. Of all these warriors who have come in every army, none of them will survive even if you refuse to fight.

33. Therefore, stand up, gain fame, conquer the enemy and enjoy an empire filled with wealth and prosperity. I have already killed them. O Savyasachi (Arjuna skilled in fighting with both hands)! You just become a medium in this war.

34. I have already killed Drona, Bhishma, Jayadratha, Karna and other war heroes. So, you kill them. Don't be afraid, fight. You must defeat the enemy in the battle.

35. Sanjaya said to Dhritarashtra: O King! On hearing these words of Keshav (Shri Krishna),

Arjuna, with folded hands and trembling, repeatedly bowed down and said to Shri Krishna with a choked throat as follows.

36. Arjuna said - O Rishikesh (Shri Krishna)! The joy that the world gets by singing your praises and the love that is generated for you is right. The demons are running away in all directions in fear and the group of Siddha Purushas are saluting You.

37. O great soul! Why shouldn't they greet you? You are a greater creator than Brahma. O Infinite, O Lord of the Gods, O Shelter of the Universe! You are immortal, you exist and whatever is beyond that is also You.

38. You are the primal deity. You are the eternal Purushottam. You are the ultimate refuge in this cosmic manifestation. You are the knower of everything, and you are the only one worth knowing. And you are the ultimate abode. O Infinite Form! This entire visible world is pervaded by You.

39. You are the omnipresent air and the law-keeping Yama, the supreme lord of death. You are the fire and also the cool, vast ocean and the moon. You are the eternal father of all. I salute you thousands of times and again and again.

40. Your power is immense, you are the master of infinite prowess, you hold everything, you are omnipresent, hence you are everything. Salutations to you from front, back and from all sides.

41-42. Knowing you as my friend and not knowing your greatness, O Krishna! Hey friend! I have called you with these addresses. Please forgive me for whatever I have done either out of foolishness or love. And many times I have insulted you while you were resting, or while eating or sitting together, sometimes alone and sometimes in front of many friends. O Infinite One who is unperturbed! Please forgive all my sins.

43. You are the father of this entire visible universe, both movable and immovable. You are the most revered and best Guru. O Lord of incomparable influence! There is no one like you in the three worlds, so how can anyone be greater than you?

44. You are the Lord to be worshipped by every living being. Therefore, I bow down before you and ask for your mercy. Just like a father tolerates the behaviour of his son, a friend tolerates the behaviour of his friend or a lover tolerates the behaviour of his beloved, similarly please tolerate my behaviour.

45. I am feeling happy seeing Your huge form which I have never seen before and at the same time my mind is filled with fear. Therefore, please be kind to me and O God of gods! O shelter of the world! Please show me your previous Purushottam Bhagavat form.

46. I wish to see Your form holding a crown, mace and discus. Oh Lord Shri Bhagvan, the thousand-armed cosmic form! Please assume your four-armed form.

47. Shri Bhagwan said- O Arjuna! Being pleased, I have, through my divine power, shown you this infinite, primordial form of the cosmic form which fills the entire universe with its radiance. No one else has seen this before except you.

48. O Arjuna, the best of the Kurus! In this human world, I cannot be seen in this form by anyone other than you - neither through the Vedas, nor through yajnas, nor through charity, nor through ritualistic actions, nor through severe austerity.

49. Do not be frightened or confused on seeing my terrible form. You leave your fear behind and be calm and then look at my familiar form.

50. Sanjaya said to Dhritarashtra: After saying this to Arjuna, Lord Vasudeva Sri Krishna showed him

His familiar form. That great souled Vishwaroop Shri Krishna assumed his gentle form and consoled the frightened Arjun.

51. O Sri Krishna, the punisher of evil people! Seeing Your gentle human form, I am now of a steady mind and have returned to my natural state.

52. Shri Bhagwan said- It is very rare to see the form of mine that you have seen. Even the deities are always eager to see that form.

53. The vision you have seen of me cannot be achieved through Vedas, nor through penance, nor through charity, nor through yajnas.

54. But, O Arjuna! Only by exclusive devotion can I be known in this form and can I be seen in person. And O Arjuna, suppressor of evil! Only through devotion can one enter my atmosphere of devotion.

55. O Pandava! He who works only for me, who considers me as the goal of his life, who worships me, who renounces attachment and who lives without hatred towards all living beings, attains me.

12. Bhakti Yoga

1. Arjuna said: Who is more accomplished among the two devotees who worship You by constantly meditating on You and those who meditate on Your imperishable, unmanifested form?

2. Sri Bhagavan said: Those who, fixing their minds on My physical form, always worship Me with devotion and utmost reverence, are considered to be the most superior in Yoga.

3-4. But those who, keeping their senses under control and maintaining equanimity everywhere, worship the firm, immovable, patient, inconceivable, omnipresent, unmanifested, indescribable, imperishable formless One, they find Me while working for the benefit of all beings.

5. Those whose mind is focused on the unmanifested formless God suffer more because the goal of the unmanifested way

can be achieved by an embodied being only through suffering.

6. But, O Partha! For those who, meditating on my physical form and dedicating all their actions to me, worship me with unwavering devotion, I quickly rescue them from the ocean of the worldly sorrow which is death.

7. Some people worship Me in My unmanifested form but due to their intellect corrupted by demonic food, they even advocate killing of those who worship My visible form. In reality, due to gross ignorance, they fight and perish with the more visible ones (fight among themselves) due to the natural law. O Arjuna! I keep these demons in terrible hell and repeatedly give them birth in the wombs of insects.

   -Nobody is different from the laws of nature.

8. O Arjun! Fix your mind on me and concentrate your intellect on me. In this way you will certainly reside in me forever.

9. If you are unable to fix your mind on Me, then O Dhananjaya Arjuna! You should have the desire to attain me through practice of Yoga.

10. If you are unable to attain Me even through practice, then make service to Me your ultimate

goal. You will attain salvation even while working for me.

11. And if You do not have the strength to perform any action, then you should make every effort to give up attachment to the fruits of all actions.

12. The path of knowledge is better than the path of practice, the path of meditation is more special than the path of knowledge, and renunciation of the fruits of action is better than the path of meditation, because by this renunciation a man immediately attains peace of mind.

13. O Arjun! People on this earth call Me by different names in different languages; some of them hate each other due to ignorance because they do not understand God.

14. O Arjun! A person who does not hate any living being, who is a friend of all and sympathetic towards all, who is devoid of ego and attachment, who remains the same in happiness and sorrow and is patient, who is adept in Yoga and is always satisfied, who controls his senses and is of firm determination, and who has surrendered his mind and intellect to Me, such a devotee of Mine is dear to Me.

15. O Arjuna, son of Kunti! The one who does not disturb people, who is not disturbed by people,

who is free from happiness, anger, jealousy and fear, that devotee is dear to me.

16. He who does not expect anything from anyone, who is pure, who is skilful in his actions, who is neutral, who is free from all worries without any suffering and who has renounced resolutions, that devotee of mine is dear to me.

17. He who does not rejoice, who does not hate, who does not worry, who does not have hopes, who renounces both good and bad, that devotional person is dear to me.

18-19. One who treats his enemy and friend alike, who is equanimous in honour and dishonour, heat and cold, pleasure and pain, who treats both praise and criticism equally, who controls his speech, who is satisfied with whatever he gets, who is not bound by any personal place and who has a steady mind, such a devotee of mine is dear to me.

20. But those devotees who reverently follow the knowledge of this immortal Dharma, recognizing Me as the Supreme Lord, are most dear to Me.

13. Kshetrakshetrajnavibhaga Yoga

Arjun said- O Keshav! I want to know what is nature and man? What is Kshetra and Kshetragya? And what is the purpose of knowledge and the knowable?

1. Sri Bhagavan said: O son of Kunti! This body is called the field, and the one who knows this field is called the knower of the field by the people having knowledge of the elements.

2. And O descendant of Bharata! Know me as the knower of the field situated in all the regions and bodies. My opinion is that the knowledge of the difference between the field and the knower of the field is true knowledge.

3. What is this Field, what is it like, how does it have disorders, where did it come from, and who is the knower of the Field and what is his power - now listen to all this from me in brief.

4. 4. Many wise sages in different Vedic mantras have repeatedly discussed this topic using different examples, in clear and logical godly statements.

5-6. Ego, intellect and the invisible nature born of it, ten senses, one mind and the five objects of the senses, desire and aversion, pleasure and pain, the aggregate of all these, the gross body, consciousness, patience - all these with their deformations are briefly called the field.

7. Humility, lack of pride, non-violence, tolerance, simplicity, service to the Guru, purity of body and mind, stability, self-control,

8. detachment from sense-objects, lack of ego, and constant awareness of birth, death, old age, disease, suffering and defects,

9. freedom from attachment and affection towards son, wife, home etc., constant equanimity towards good and bad events,

10. continuous and unquestionable devotion towards me, desire to stay in a solitary place, disinterest in joining the crowd,

11. constant awareness of the knowledge related to the soul and self-realization – I declare all these as knowledge. And whatever is opposite to all these is ignorance.

12. I will now share with you something that, when understood, can lead to achieving eternal life and salvation. He is the 'Param Brahma' - that which has no beginning; He can neither be called true nor unreal. (He is beyond the truth and untruth of the material world)

13. His hands and feet are everywhere; his eyes, head and face are everywhere; his ears are in all directions; the Supreme Brahma is omnipresent and present in this universe.

14. He is aware of the qualities of all the senses, yet He is devoid of senses and detached from everything. However, He is carrying them all. He is beyond the material modes of nature, yet he is the enjoyer of the modes.

15. He is outside and inside all beings. He is dynamic and also static. He is so subtle that they cannot be known. He is far and also near.

16. The Supreme Being is undivided and exists in one form, yet He appears to be divided into all beings. It should be understood that He protects all living beings, destroys them and then creates them afresh.

17. He is the light of all luminous things, He is beyond darkness. He is the knowledge, He is the one worth knowing, and what is gained

from knowledge is also He. He is present in everyone's heart.

18. Thus I have explained in brief about the Field, Knowledge and the Known (God). By knowing this my devotee becomes worthy of attaining my nature.

19. Know both nature and man as eternal. Consider that disorders and qualities have originated from nature.

20. Nature is said to be the cause of action and cause, and man is the cause of experiencing happiness and sorrow.

21. The man residing in nature enjoys the qualities arising from nature, and attachment to these qualities becomes the cause of his birth in superior and inferior species.

22. There is another Supreme Person residing in this body, who is called the all-witnessing, permitting, sustaining, consuming Maheshwara Paramatma.

23. A person who understands the Purusha and the Guna-filled nature in this way does not take rebirth even though he performs all kinds of actions.

24. Some people see God within themselves through meditation, some through the practice

of knowledge and there are some who see God within themselves through selfless Karma Yoga.

25. Some other people, despite not knowing these paths, worship God by hearing about Him from others and by having faith in Him and by being devoted to Him. They, too, transcend death.

26. O best of the descendants of Bharata! Know this that whatever movable or immovable thing is created is created by the conjunction of the field and the knower of the field, that is, by the conjunction of nature and man.

27. One who perceives the eternal Supreme Being within all temporary beings without being disturbed, and recognizes that the Supreme Being remains unaffected even when these beings perish, is the one who truly understands.

28. The man who sees God everywhere and in all living beings with equal respect does not corrupt himself through his soul. In this way, he attains the ultimate salvation.

29. Everywhere it is Nature that performs actions - he who understands this and therefore knows the Self as non-doer, he alone truly knows.

30. When a person sees that all living beings, despite their separate existence, are situated in the one Brahma and hence considers the entire

expanse to have originated from Him, then he attains the realization of Brahma.

31. O Arjuna, son of Kunti! Since this indestructible Supreme Being is eternal and attributeless, even while residing in the body, He neither performs any action nor is involved in it.

32. This sky, being subtle and omnipresent, is not affected by anything. Similarly, the soul situated in the Brahma vision, even while situated in the body, is not attached to the body.

33. O Bharata! Just as the Sun alone illuminates the entire universe, similarly the soul (Kshetrajna) situated in the body illuminates the entire body (Kshetra).

34. He who, through the eye of knowledge, knows the difference between the Field and the knower of the Field, and the method of liberation of beings from the bondage of nature, attains Brahma.

14. Gunatrayavibhaga Yoga

1. The Lord said: Now I shall narrate to you again this supreme knowledge, which is the best of all knowledge; after knowing which all the sages have attained the supreme perfection.

2. Those who have taken shelter of this knowledge and have attained a divine nature like mine, do not have to take birth even when the time of creation comes and do not have to suffer when the time of destruction comes.

3. O Bharata! Mahad Brahma i.e. Prakriti is my womb which I impregnate and from it all living beings are born.

4. O Arjuna, son of Kunti! The place of origin of all the living beings which are born in all the wombs is my nature and I am the father-man who sows the seed in it.

5. O mighty-armed Arjuna! Sattva (goodness), Rajas (charge) and Tamas (inactivity)- these

three qualities have arisen from nature and they bind the immortal soul to the body.

6. Among these, the Sattva Guna (goodness) being pure, is the illuminator of pure knowledge and heals the mind; and O sinless Arjuna! It binds the body to the soul because of the desire to be creative and acquire good knowledge.

7. Rajoguna (passion), being the form of passion, is the root of never-ending aspirations and cravings. O Arjuna, son of Kunti! It binds the soul with the body in the bond of fruitive actions.

8. O Bharata! Tamoguna (inactivity) arises from ignorance. It attracts the embodied being to attachments and binds him to the body in the snare of negligence, laziness and sleep.

9. O Bharata! Goodness, i.e. Sattva Guna makes the soul associated with peace and happiness, Rajoguna makes one associated with fruitive actions, and Tamoguna covers up knowledge and makes one associated with negligence.

10. O Bharata! When the influence of Rajas and Tamas is reduced, Sattva becomes effective. When the influence of Sattva and Tamas decreases, Rajas becomes effective and when

the influence of Sattva and Rajas decreases, the influence of Tamas increases.

11. When the light of good knowledge emerges in this body with the cooperation of all the senses, then it can be understood that the influence of Sattva Guna is increasing.

12. O Arjuna, the best of Bharatas! When the influence of Rajoguna increases, then symptoms of excessive attachment, greed, beginning of heinous deeds, unrest and uncontrolled desires appear.

13. O Kurunandana Arjuna! When Tamoguna increases, ignorance, inactivity, negligence and attachment arise.

14. When a person gives up his physical body while being under the influence of Sattva Guna, then he goes to the holy world of the great souls who have attained the knowledge of God.

15. When one dies under the influence of the mode of passion, he is born among those attached to the fruits of their actions, and one who dies under the influence of the mode of ignorance is born in the womb of a fool.

16. The result of good deeds performed under the influence of Sattva Guna is Sattvic and pure. The result of the work done in Rajoguna

is sorrow and the result of the work done in Tamoguna is foolishness and ignorance.

17. True knowledge arises from the mode of Sattva Guna. Greed arises from Rajoguna, and negligence, infatuation and ignorance arise from Tamoguna.

18. Sattvik persons keep rising upwards; Rajasiks stay in the middle and Tamasiks keep falling downwards by indulging in wrong deeds.

19. When the wise man sees that there is no doer other than the modes of nature and knows the Supreme Being beyond these modes, then he attains My divine nature.

20. By rising above those qualities which arise from association with the body, the embodied being becomes free from the sufferings of birth, death and old age and attains the supremely blissful eternal life, i.e. salvation.

21. Arjuna spoke - O Lord! What are the characteristics of the one who rises above these three qualities? What is his behaviour like? And how can he go beyond these three modes of nature?

22-25. The Lord said, O Arjuna, son of Pandu! A person who remains unaffected by knowledge, proneness, and attachments and doesn't desire in the absence of these understanding that actions are driven by nature and staying neutral and unwavering. They remain indifferent to pleasure and pain and remain healthy, concentrating in his soul, treats soil, stone, gold the same, remain indifferent on receiving dear or unpleasant materials and remain calm in all situations, whether receiving praise or criticism, honor or insult, has similar intentions towards friends or enemies and who has renounced starts of all material activities. This person is called Gunatita, having risen above the influence of modes of nature.

26. He who is devoted to Me with exclusive devotion, transcends these modes of nature and rises to the state of Brahma.

27. And I am the state of Brahma, I am the state of eternal salvation. In the same way, I am the eternal righteousness and the state of supreme happiness.

15. Purushottama Yoga

1. Sri Bhagavan said - It is said as a parable that in this material world there is a Peepal tree whose roots are upwards, branches downwards and the leaves are verses of knowledge. One who understands this is the knower of the Vedas.

2. The branches of the Peepal tree, which have grown by the touch of the qualities of nature and are in the form of objects, move up and down. Its roots which bind karma are spread deep in the human world.

3-4. Thus, the actual form of this tree is not visible here. It has no beginning, no end and its base is not visible. Man should cut down this strong-rooted Peepal tree with the strong weapon of detachment and pray that I take refuge in the original man, the founder of that religion, who has spread the eternal tendency of the world. Seeking the ultimate position is the goal, with the attainment of it leading to freedom from the cycle of birth and death.

5. Those who are free from the feelings of pride and delusion, who have got rid of the defects caused by attachment to the fruits of actions, who are always absorbed in eternal spiritual knowledge, whose senses have become tranquil, who are free from the dualities of pleasure and pain and are devoid of stupidity. Such wise saints attain the ultimate indestructible position.

6. A place that doesn't need the sun, moon or fire to give light; a place where one does not have to be reborn - that is my supreme abode.

7. A section of my being, which is now eternal is in constant conflict with my five senses and the sixth sense, the mind due to conditioned life living within nature.

8. This part of me (part of God) in the form of a living being, takes the senses along with the mind from one body to another in the same manner as air moves from one place to another along with fragrances.

9. Thus, taking another body, the soul enjoys its natural objects by using its ears, eyes, touch (skin), tongue, nose and mind.

10. A foolish person cannot see the part of God who abandons the body or stays in it or enjoys the pleasures of the body under the influence of the modes of nature. But the wise with the eyes of knowledge see all this.

11. Yogis, who have achieved self-realization through effort in spiritual practice, see God within themselves. But one who has not achieved self-realization, such foolish people, despite trying, are unable to see God within themselves.

12. The light that is in the Sun, which removes the darkness of the entire world, and the light that is in the Moon and the fire, consider that to be my light.

13. Entering the earth, I sustain all living beings with my power, and becoming the light that produces the essence, I nourish all vegetation.

14. Taking shelter in the bodies of living beings and becoming the fire of life-gastric fire, I digest four types of food through the vital air and the apana air.

15. And I am situated in everyone's heart; from Me come memory and knowledge and their destruction. In fact, I am the one who can be known through all the Vedas. I am the knower

of the Vedas, and I am also the one who reveals the Vedas.

16. There are two in this body, perishable and indestructible. All living beings are destructible and the one who remains constant among them, the inner controller, is indestructible.

17. In addition to these beings, there is the ultimate form of God, who is indestructible. This indestructible Supreme Being enters the three worlds and nourishes them.

18. Because I am beyond mortals and superior to the imperishable, I am famous in all the Vedas and the worlds by the name of Purushottama.

19. O Bharata! One who, without any attachment, knows the Supreme Personality of God in this manner, is sure to know everything and he worships me with complete devotion.

20. O sinless Arjuna! I have told you the most secret knowledge. O Bharata! Knowing this, man should become intelligent and make his life successful by fulfilling his duties.

16. Devasurasampadvibhaga Yoga

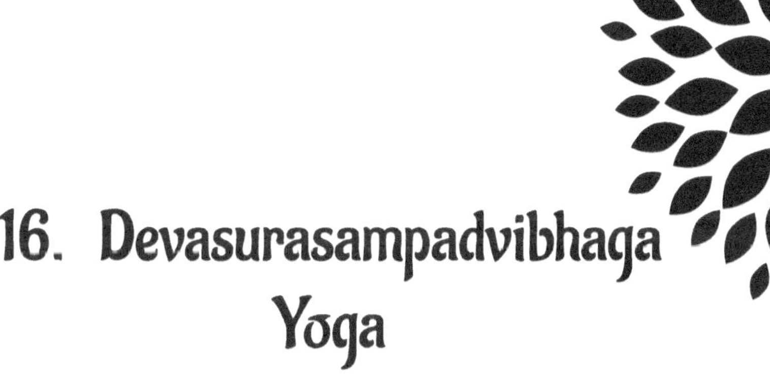

1. The Lord said: Fearlessness, purity of consciousness, devotion to spiritual knowledge and yoga, charity, self-restraint, devotion to yajna, self-study, penance and simplicity

2. non-violence, truthfulness, absence of anger, sacrifice, peace, disinterest in finding faults in others, kindness to living beings, absence of greed, decency, dignity and steadfastness

3. Brightness, forgiveness, patience, purity, absence of malice, freedom from the desire for honour – O Bharata! All these divine qualities are present in the one who is born with the divine nature.

4. O Partha! Hypocrisy, pride, arrogance, anger, harshness and ignorance are found in those born with demonic qualities.

5. Divine quality is considered to be liberating and demonic quality is considered to have bondage. O Pandava! Don't worry, because you are born with divine qualities.

6. There are two types of creation in this world – divine and demonic. And O Partha! I have described the divine nature to you in detail. Now listen to me describing the demonic nature.

7. Those having demonic nature neither know the inclination towards action nor the retirement from action. Neither purity nor morality nor sense of truth is found in them.

8. They say that this world is false; it has no basis and it is not regulated by any God. He says that it arises from libido, and there is no other cause than that.

9. By firmly adopting this viewpoint, the enemies of the world, doers of the terrible deeds, the demonic people of little knowledge, who have lost their self-knowledge, are born for the destruction of the world.

10. Under the influence of foolish, never-ending desires, arrogant, proud and demonic people make evil resolutions and are inclined to carry out evil desires.

11-12. Taking shelter in such excessive worry that never ends till death, the ultimate enjoyers of sensual pleasures, determining that 'pleasure is everything', by marrying more and producing more children, trapped in the net of hundreds of hopes, desire to unjustly accumulate power and wealth for lustful, wrathful and sensual pleasures.

13-15. Today I have achieved this, now I will fulfill this desire, I have this much wealth and power, then in the future this much more will be mine,

I have killed this enemy and I will kill other enemies as well. I am God. I am all-powerful. I am the one who enjoys. I am perfect. I am strong and happy.

I am rich and born in a high family, who else is like me? I will perform a yajna, I will give in charity and I will have a great time - people stupefied by ignorance say such things.

16. Those who are deluded by many thoughts, caught in the net of stupidity and addicted to the satisfaction of sensual pleasures, fall into the impure hell.

17. These demonic people, who think themselves to be superior, who are arrogant and obsessed with wealth and false prestige, and who are

full of pride, sometimes, out of arrogance and without following the rites and ceremonies, perform sacrifices for the sake of name only and desire to eat the food of others' sacrifices for free.

18. Under the influence of ego, power, pride, lust and anger, these hateful people envy Me who resides in their own and other people's bodies.

19. I always send these vile, hateful, cruel and evil-doers to demonic births in this ocean of existence.

20. O son of Kunti! By being born again and again in demonic wombs and not finding Me, the foolish creatures keep falling towards the lowest state.

21. There are three gates to hell that destroy the soul: lust, anger and greed. Therefore, man must give up these three.

    Greed = Desire for more results than what you have done

22. O son of Kunti! A person who escapes from these three types of hell-gates works for the welfare of the soul and thus gradually attains the ultimate salvation.

23. A man who, abandoning the injunctions of the scriptures, voluntarily indulges in pleasures,

attains neither success nor happiness and thus neither the ultimate salvation.

24. Therefore, one must understand what is duty and what is non-duty as per the injunctions of the scriptures. Knowing the rules mentioned in the scriptures, it is appropriate for you to perform your duties here in this world.

17. Shraddhatrayavibhaga Yoga

1. Arjuna said- O Krishna! What is the position of those who do worship, sacrifice, duties, etc. according to their own wishes with faith without following the scriptural rituals, i.e., manners? Are they Sattvic, Rajoguni or Tamoguni?

2. Shri Bhagwan said: According to the nature of living beings, they can have three types of faith. - Sattvik, Rajasik and Tamasi. Now hear from me about this.

3. O Bharata! Some degree of faith develops in a person from the understanding gained from his past experiences in various situations. A person's qualities are expressed according to his faith.

4. Sattvik men worship gods, Rajasik men worship Yakshas and demons and the other Tamasik men worship ghosts and spirits.

5-6. Those foolish men, who are arrogant and egoistic and who, driven by lust and passion, perform severe austerities contrary to the scriptures, torment the five elements of the body as well as Me present in the conscience. You should consider such people to be having demonic resolve.

7. Food is also loved in three ways. Similarly, yajnas, penance, and charity are also dear in three ways. Now listen about their differences.

8. Sattvika people like food that increases longevity, purifies life, enhances strength, health, happiness and gaiety, is flavorful, non-oily, nutritious and tasty.

9. Spicy, sour, salty, very hot, pungent, dry, acidic foods are loved by Rajasik people and such food causes misery, grief and disease.

10. Food that has been lying for a long time, tasteless, smelly, stale, dirty, impure is loved by Tamasi people.

11. A yajna performed with full concentration and as per the prescribed rituals, considering it as a duty without any desire for fruit, is called Sattvik.

12. O Bharatashrestha! The sacrifice which is performed with the sole purpose of getting

results and for display, should be considered as Rajasi.

13. The yagna which is performed without following the scriptures, without distributing prasad, without chanting Vedic mantras, without giving dakshina to the priests and without faith is considered to be Tamasi.

14. Worship of Gods, Brahmins, Gurus and learned men done with purity, simplicity, celibacy and non-violence - this is called physical austerity.

15. Practice of truth, loving, beneficial words and spiritual texts that do not cause pain- This is called the austerity of speech.

16. Cheerfulness of mind, gentle feeling, silence, control of mind, self-control, purification of emotions - this is called mental austerity.

17. When these three kinds of austerity are performed by a person with equanimity and with complete devotion, renouncing any desire for results, it is called Sattvika austerity.

18. The penance which is performed to gain honour, respect or prestige or for the sake of display is called Rajasik penance. It is neither stable nor fixed.

19. The austerity which is performed out of foolishness by tormenting oneself and with

the intent to destroy or harm others is called Tamasi.

20. The charity which is given as a duty, at the right place, at the right time to the right person without any expectation of anything in return, is considered to be Sattvik.

21. But the charity which is given for a reward or with the hope of some future benefit and which is painful to give, is called Rajasik charity.

22. Charity given disrespectfully and with contempt without considering the right place, right time and the right person is called Tamasi.

23. Since the beginning of creation, these three words Om Tat Sat have been used to indicate that 'Brahma is truth'. For this, Brahmagyani, Vedas and Yajna were created.

24. Thus the Brahmins always perform the rituals of sacrifice, charity and penance by chanting Om.

25. Without desiring the fruit of action, a man should perform various types of sacrifices, austerities and donations by saying the word 'Tat'. The purpose of such divine activities is to attain liberation from the bondage of life.

26. The word 'Sat' is used in the sense of reality and goodness and O Partha! The word 'sat' is also used for auspicious deeds.

27. To remain firmly steadfast in yajna, austerity and charity is also called 'Sat' and the action done for this is also called 'Sat'.

28. O Partha! The yajnas, alms, penance, etc. which are performed without faith are perishable. That is called unreal and there is no benefit from it either in this world or the next.

18. Sanyasa Yoga

1. Arjuna said- O mighty-armed Krishna! O Hrishikesh! O the killer of demon Keshi! I want to know the separate mystery of Sanyasa and renunciation.

2. Sri Bhagavan said: Wise people call the renunciation of actions motivated by desire as Sanyasa. Wise people call the renunciation of attachment to the fruits of all actions as renunciation.

3. Some thoughtful men say that action alone is to be abandoned because it is flawed. But other scholars believe that the acts of yajna, charity and austerity should never be abandoned.

4. O the best of Bharata! Now listen to my decision regarding this renunciation. O male

tiger! Sacrifice has been described to be of three kinds.

5. The acts of yajna, charity and austerity should never be abandoned, but must be continued. Undoubtedly, yajnas, charity and austerities purify even the great souls.

6. But these actions too must be performed without attachment and desire for results. O Partha! This is certainly my best intention.

7. One should never abandon one's assigned duties. If someone, under the influence of attachment, abandons his prescribed duties, such abandonment is considered Tamasi.

8. The person who renounces the prescribed duties because he considers them troublesome or out of fear of bodily suffering commits a Rajasik renunciation and hence, he does not get the fruits of this renunciation.

9. O Arjuna! The renunciation of a person who abandons all material association and attachment to the fruit of his actions and does his duty as he considers it to be a "must do" is considered to be Sattvik.

10. A wise renunciant, free from doubts and having a Sattvik feeling, does not abhor an inconvenient duty and does not get absorbed in a convenient duty.

11. It is undoubtedly impossible for any embodied being to completely renounce action; but he who renounces attachment to the fruit of action is called a renunciant.

12. Those who have not renounced, after death they receive three kinds of results of their actions – pleasant, unpleasant and mixed. But those who have renounced it do not have to suffer the joys and sorrows of such consequences.

13. O mighty-armed Arjuna! Now listen to me about the five reasons given in Sankhya Shastra for performing actions.

14. The place of karma is the body, the doer, various senses, various types of efforts and the fifth god.

15. Whatever right or wrong a man does with his body, speech and mind, there are these five causes for it.

16. In such a condition, the person who, due to his uncultured intellect, believes himself to be the doer, (owing to the imperfection of his intellect) is unable to understand what the truth is.

17. He who has no ego and whose intellect is not impure does not kill the world even while killing it and he does not get bound by his actions.

18. Knowledge, the object of knowledge and the knower of knowledge - these three are the reasons that motivate action. Similarly, karma, senses and the doer - these three are the components of karma.

   The one who acquires knowledge becomes the doer of an action through the senses. This is the collection karma.

19. According to the qualities of nature, there are three kinds of knowledge, action and doer. Now listen to me as I share these three types as it is described in the Sankhya philosophy of qualities.

   [Three types of knowledge]

20. The knowledge by which one and the same undivided, indestructible being is seen in all the living beings divided in various forms, consider that knowledge as Sattvik knowledge.

21. The knowledge by which different divided feelings are visible in all the living beings divided in various forms, consider that knowledge as Rajasik knowledge.

22. But the knowledge which considers one action as everything and does not pay any attention to its reason and does not understand its real

meaning, which is narrow mind - that is called Tamasi knowledge.

[Three Kinds of Karma]

23. Action which is prescribed without attachment and love-hate and without desire for the fruit of its action is called Sattvika.

24. That work which is done with the desire for results and for enjoyment, with hard work and with a feeling of false ego, is called Rajas.

25. The work which is started under the influence of attachment, without thinking about the result, loss, violence against others and one's own strength, is called Tamasi Karma.

[Three types of doers]

26. The doer who is free from attachment, who does not speak egotistically, who has patience and enthusiasm and who is not perturbed by success or failure is called a Sattvic doer.

27. The doer who, due to excessive attachment to the action and its results, is eager to obtain the fruits of his actions, is avaricious, causes pain to others, is impure, and is agitated by rejoicing or lamenting, is called Rajasi.

28. He who is disorganised, uncultured, stubborn, deceitful, adept at insulting others, is always unhappy, procrastinates and takes time to complete every task is called a doer in the mode of Tamoguna.

29. O Dhananjaya Arjuna! I will explain to you in detail the three types of wisdom and patience, each one separately, according to the modes of nature. Listen to those.

    [Three types of intelligence]

30. The intelligence which understands to start action and retirement. That which understands what is to be done and what is not, what is to be feared and what is not, what binds the soul and what is liberating, O Partha! That intellect is Satvik.

31. The intellect by which a man misunderstands Dharma and Adharma, the doable and the undoable, O Partha! That intelligence is Rajasik.

32. O Partha! The intellect which, under the influence of delusion and ignorance, believes unrighteousness to be righteousness and always sees the opposite of the truth, is a Tamasi intellect.

    [Three types of Dhriti (patience = stability of attention)]

33. O Partha! The single-minded Dhriti with which a man keeps the actions of his mind, soul and senses steady and balanced is Sattvik Dhriti.

34. O Partha! The dhriti with which a man, with a desire for results, holds Dharma, Artha and Kama with attachment, is Rajasik Dhriti.

35. O Partha! The Dhriti due to which a foolish man is unable to give up dreams, fear, grief, despair and pride. That is Tamasi Dhriti.

[Three types of happiness]

36. O the best of Bharata! Now listen to me describing the three types of happiness. The practice of which keeps a person happy and which ends his suffering.

37. That which appears like poison in the beginning but results in nectar; that which arises from the joy of Self-knowledge, is called Sattvika happiness.

38. The pleasure which is derived through the senses from the contact of their objects and which is like nectar in the beginning but is like poison in the end is called Rajoguni (pleasure).

39. The happiness which keeps the soul confused both in the beginning and the end, which

arises from sleep, laziness and negligence, is called Tamasi happiness.

[Nature of Varnas as determined by Swadharma (duty)]

40. There is no one, either on this earth or among the deities in heaven, who is free from these three qualities born of nature.

Chapter 4, Divine Saying 13

Srimad Bhagavad Gita is the best and most accepted book. Therefore, this is the parable and the main basis for understanding the Manusmriti and other texts.

Classification of caste was considered on the basis of qualities and duty. Errors creep into any rule or thing over a period of time. Now on the basis of those errors, if someone behaves in the society on the basis of the family in which he was born then such people do not get the wisdom to attain the highest salvation. Because their minds are influenced by flawed thinking. If one wants to attain the highest ultimate destination, he must completely remove the caste-based surname acquired on the basis of birth in a family to eliminate the influence of wrong thinking on his mind. In today's time, there are many types of duties in society based on self-quality, in such a situation they can use a surname related to their present work.

41. O Arjuna, conqueror of enemies! The duties of Brahmins, Kshatriyas, Vaishyas and Shudras have also been divided on the basis of their inherent qualities.

42. Peace-lovingness, self-control, austerity, purity, forbearance, truthfulness, knowledge, experience and faith in God - these are the self-qualities by which a brahmin performs his duties.

43. Courageousness, brilliance, patience, efficiency, not turning away in the midst of battle, charity and leadership- these are the self-qualities of a Kshatriya.

44. Agriculture, cow protection and business - these are the self-qualities of a Vaishya. And the self-quality of a Shudra is to serve.

45. A person engaged in his duty according to self-quality attains salvation. Now you hear from me how this happens.

46. The one who worships the Supreme Being, due to whom all beings are born and who is omnipresent, while performing his duties, his life becomes successful and he gets salvation.

47. Doing one's duty according to one's own quality, even if it is done incorrectly, is better than doing someone else's work well. A person who performs his duties according to his quality does not commit any sin.

48. O son of Kunti! Even if the duty arising from one's own quality is flawed, one should not abandon it. Just like smoke is associated with fire, similarly defects are present in all works.

49. Who has removed attachment from everywhere. He who has no desires left, who has conquered his mind, attains the highest perfect state of freedom from the consequences of his actions through the practice of renunciation.

50. O son of Kunti! I will briefly describe to you how a person who has attained this siddhi attains the ultimate siddha state, i.e., Brahma, which is the state of supreme knowledge. Listen to it.

51-53. Purified by his good intelligence and patiently controlling the mind, renouncing the objects of sense-gratification, free from attachment and aversion, he who lives in a solitary place, who eats little, who controls his body, mind and speech, who is always in meditation and Yoga, and who is completely detached, who is free from false ego, false power, false pride, lust, anger and the feeling of accumulating material things, who is free from the sense of false ownership and is tranquil - he certainly becomes fit to attain Brahmabhaav (State of Brahma).

54. Having attained Brahmabhaav, a happy man neither grieves nor desires anything. Considering all living beings as equal, one attains supreme devotion to me.

55. Through devotion he comes to know God as He is, what He is and who He is. And thus, having known me truly, he remains in his devotion to me.

56. My pure devotee, under My shelter, while engaged in all kinds of activities, attains by My grace an eternal and indestructible position.

57. Surrender all your actions in your mind to Me, considering Me as God, and practising the stability of your intellect, keep your thoughts constantly focused on Me.

58. If you concentrate on me, you will cross all mountains of difficulties with my grace. But if you are overcome by ego and do not do as I say, you will be destroyed.

59. If, under the influence of ego, you think, 'I will not fight', then your resolve is useless. Nature will force you (to do your duty).

60. O son of Kunti! Whatever duty you do not want to perform under the influence of attachment, you will do it forcibly due to being bound by your own quality

61. O Arjuna! God resides in the heart of all living beings and with the power of His Maya, He makes them all rotate like a pot mounted on a wheel.

62. O Bharata! You must seek refuge in God with your entire being. By his grace you will attain supreme peace and immortality.

63. Thus have I explained to you the most profound knowledge. Think about all this carefully and do whatever you like.

64. And now listen to this most profound supreme word of mine. You are very dear to me, so I will tell you about your welfare.

65. Concentrate your mind on me, become my devotee, perform yajnas for me, salute me. You will attain me only, this is my true promise, because you are dear to me.

66. Abandoning all religions, take refuge only in me. I will free you from all sins. Don't be sad.

67. You should never impart all this knowledge to one who is not an ascetic, who is not a

devotee, who does not want to listen and who hates me.

68. He who imparts this most secret knowledge to my devotees will undoubtedly find me due to his supreme devotion to me.

69. I have no devotee more beloved than him among humans, and there is none on earth who is dearer to me than him.

70. And he who practises this dialogue of ours will worship Me by yajna, this is my opinion.

71. And he who will only listen with devotion and without malice will also attain salvation and reach that auspicious world where the virtuous dwell.

72. O Partha! Did you listen to all this attentively? Hey Dhananjaya! Has the attachment which you developed due to ignorance been destroyed?

73. Arjuna said: O Achyut Krishna! By your grace my attachment has been destroyed and my memory has been restored. Now my doubts are gone and I am stable. Now I will do as you say.

74. Sanjay said: Thus, I hear the thrilling conversation between Vasudeva Sri Krishna and the great soul Arjuna.

75. By the grace of Vyasa, I heard the most profound knowledge of Yoga as told by the mouth of Lord Krishna, the Lord of Yoga.

76. O King! I feel blessed by repeatedly recalling this wonderful and sacred dialogue between Keshav (Shri Krishna) and Arjuna.

77. O King! By repeatedly remembering that wonderful form of Hari (Lord Sri Krishna) I am becoming very amazed and feeling blissful again and again.

78. Where there is Sri Krishna, the lord of yoga, and Arjuna, the archer, there is prosperity, victory, glory and unshakable morality, this is my opinion.

Jai Sri krishna

notes

notes

notes

notes

notes

notes

notes

notes

notes

notes

notes

notes

notes

notes

notes

notes

notes

notes